A Walk with
THE BLACK
MOSES

*Sandy Stephens' Inspiring Stories
of Hope and Determination —*
How You Too Can Aspire to a Legacy of Greatness

Barbara R. Stephens Foster

A WALK WITH THE BLACK MOSES
SANDY STEPHENS' INSPIRING STORIES OF HOPE
AND DETERMINATION — HOW YOU TOO CAN
ASPIRE TO A LEGACY OF GREATNESS

iUniverse books may be ordered through booksellers or by contacting:

iUniverse
1663 Liberty Drive
Bloomington, IN 47403
www.iuniverse.com
1-800-Authors (1-800-288-4677)

Because of the dynamic nature of the Internet, any web addresses or links contained in this book may have changed since publication and may no longer be valid. The views expressed in this work are solely those of the author and do not necessarily reflect the views of the publisher, and the publisher hereby disclaims any responsibility for them.

Credit to the National Football Foundation for the use of Sandy Stephens' 2011 College Football Hall of Fame plaque on the book cover.

ISBN: 978-1-5320-7896-5 (sc)
ISBN: 978-1-5320-7897-2 (e)

Library of Congress Control Number: 2019910347

Print information available on the last page.

iUniverse rev. date: 08/02/2019

Thank you, Sandy, for your love and inspiration.

CONTENTS

ACKNOWLEDGMENTS

Thank you to my siblings and children for providing unconditional love and unwavering support as I focused on completion of this project. Ray Stephens, Joyce Bell, Lee Stephens, and Sharla Foster, I love you dearly. Gratitude is what I feel for Otis Courtney and Sunil Shrestha who provided their time, talent, and resources during the past three years. My forever friend Mary Ellen Gee brought her considerable proofreading skills to my aide when I needed them the most. The book is a reality thanks to her caring appraisal. Thank you to the staff of District 279 for their years of patience and belief in me and the work.

I am forever indebted to the original Book Believers Group (BBG) led in 2009 by the now deceased Catherine Attaway, Charlie Sanders, Dan Pothier, and Dr. Jeanne T. Lupton. They were joined in the BBG journey by Gene Huey, Miles Cohen, Jocelyn & Terry Gloster, Dr. David V. Taylor, Otis Courtney, Ezell Jones, L. Jeannette & Pierpont Mobley, and John Moorman. The BBG gave the book the financial support needed to start the process.

Without the reflections and insights of the survey contributors, Sandy's legacy could not be brought to life. Special thanks to: Catherine Attaway, Stephen Allen, George Bell, Ralph Bell, Walter A. Bowser, David Butwin, Miles Cohen, Otis Courtney, Barry Dillard, David Ekstrand, Kenneth Finney Jr. (deceased), Jocelyn Gloster, Terry Gloster, Milton Harrison, Melvin Hickenbottom, Terry Hitchcock, Andrea Hjelm, Martha (Martie) Hudson, Lou Hudson (deceased), Gene Huey, Benjamin Mchie, Angie McLee, Charles McLee, Dan Pothier, John Robinson, Gen. Dennis Schulstad, Dominique Sims, Clyde Thomas, Dr. John M. Williams (deceased), and Clifford Wilson.

Heartfelt thanks to the new BBG members who provided financial support in 2017-2019: Gaysha Anderson, Kimberly Bell, Reece Bell, Rojanne Brown, Joe & Krista Cassidy, Bruce Challgren, PaviElle French, Lonnie Gillian, Sigrid Gray, Patty Hoag, Hillary Jeffries, Bonnie Johnson, Carla & Ken Johnson, Tiffanee & Michael Jules, Raleigh Kaminsky,

Jennifer Leslie, George Meissner, Raymond Parson, Linda Royal, Maureen Skramstad, Bonnie Spivak, Dr. Tommy Watson, Deb Will, Patricia & Ron Whyte, Clifford Wilson, and Serena & John Wright.

To you all, God loves you and so do I.

Sandy received a high school graduation card that had the entire **IF** poem on it. The poem spoke to his spirit and much of Sandy's approach to life is reflected in the excerpt chosen. As his life journey continued and circumstances occurred that tested his resolve, Sandy discovered **INVICTUS**. **INVICTUS** seemed to take the knowledge shared in the Kipling poem to the next level for Sandy. "My head is bloody, but unbowed," was Sandy's mantra for the remainder of his life.

IF

Rudyard Kipling, 1865-1936
If you can keep your head when all about you
    Are losing theirs and blaming it on you;
If you can trust yourself when all men doubt you,
    But make allowance for their doubting, too;
If you can wait and not be tired by waiting,
    Or, being lied about, don't deal in lies,
Or, being hated, don't give way to hating,
    And yet don't look too good, nor talk too wise;
. . .
If you can talk with crowds and keep your virtue,
    Or walk with kings—not lose the common touch;
If neither foes nor loving friends can hurt you;
    If all men count with you, but none too much;
If you can fill the unforgiving minute
    With sixty seconds' worth of distance run—
Yours is the Earth and everything that's in it,
    And—which is more—you'll be a Man, my son!

INVICTUS

William Ernest Henley, 1849-1903

. . .

In the fell clutch of circumstance
    I have not winced nor cried aloud.
Under the bludgeoning of chance
    My head is bloody, but unbowed.

. . .

It matters not how strait the gate,
    How charged with punishments the scroll.
I am the master of my fate:
    I am the captain of my soul.

INTRODUCTION

Sanford E. Stephens II attended the University of Minnesota in 1958 when first-year football players were not on the varsity team. They served in the role of opponent in scrimmages and were used to sharpen the skills of the players on the third and fourth varsity squads. The Minnesota Athletic Department asked Sanford for a nickname to use for future publicity purposes. He offered "Sandy" because Sanford sounded too proper to his ear. Furthermore, childhood nicknames, while amusing in his youth, were unacceptable to carry into the future he envisioned for himself.

The athletic department staff were surprised by what happened when Sandy and his teammates performed in front of a packed house of students, staff, and community supporters the first time they scrimmaged in Memorial Stadium. The crowd was excited to see if the new recruits from Pennsylvania could live up to the acclaim of Coach Warmath and the assistant coaches. After the scrimmage, *Minnesota Daily* sports reporter David Butwin headed his column "Sandy Stephens Day"[1] as praise for the extraordinary performance of Sandy and the new varsity players. From that day forward, Sandy was the nickname that was recognized in the athletic community, accepted by family and friends, used easily by teammates, and remembered by coaches, sports writers, fans and others. It will be the primary identifier used in these pages. I introduce the book with an explanation of his name because Sandy Stephens is a legendary figure in the annals of Black quarterbacks in college football. His name is synonymous with leadership, hope, determination, intelligence, and inspiration.

Sandy Stephens was named the first Black man to earn consensus All-American quarterback recognition at a Division 1 university in 1961. His ability to reach such status in the 1960s era of the civil rights movement was groundbreaking. Sandy's dream of publishing an autobiography started in 1984 when he was 44 years old. The original working title for the book was, *Dandy Sandy, Triple Threat +1, 1ˢᵗ Black All-American Quarterback.* Sandy lived life to the fullest in the years leading up to authoring a book. Consequently, the original book outline included twenty-one chapter headings. He was poised to flesh out the topics listed under the headings with the intention to provide a compelling chronicle of his life and athletic career. While he spent as much time as possible recording the details of the outline, he sought ways to attract financial support to give himself the means to work full time on the project. Unfortunately, he was unsuccessful in gaining the foothold he needed to progress quickly. He worked on various pieces of his vision with numerous friends and potential promoters, but nothing clicked. Years passed and life went on but Sandy remained determined to fulfill his dream.

By 1999, when our collaboration started, Sandy had compressed the book outline headings into five themes and seven chapters. He and I made multiple lists of potential titles for his book. We were looking for something that we felt would grab the attention of the reader and capture the meaning of the book. One of those possibilities was *Minnsylvanian*. It was a term he created while preparing for one of his presentations to a University of Minnesota class. We did not settle on using Minnsylvanian in the book title, but the term describes us well. Our family's contemporary story is undeniably interwoven between Pennsylvania (PA) and Minnesota (MN). The "Minn" is first in the term because a representative number of us have lived in Minnesota longer than we lived in Pennsylvania.

Eventually we settled on the working title given in this excerpt of the draft:

The story we are about to delve into has probably been argued, debated, and bet on since the late 1950s. There have been so called "taboos" regarding the positions of quarterback, center, and middle linebacker in professional football, but no one has written about them from an insider's perspective. Black men in these positions were certainly unheard of during the 1950s and most of the 1960s in pro football. In the working title, *Sanford (Sandy) Stephens to the Mountain: Quarterback Dreams*, an examination of the struggles of a Black quarterback through my eyes and experiences will reveal many areas of the struggles that have only been talked about in Black communities in almost every bar, barbershop, and pool hall. . . . My experiences leave me feeling like the Moses of Black quarterbacks—able to

see the promised land, but unable to enter it. **Sandy Stephens,**
1999

It wasn't long before completing the book also became my dream and passion. Sandy and I reviewed the volumes of book material he and others had prepared. He shared new details of his life with me and I was able to gain a deeper understanding of some of his challenges and triumphs. We were always close, but an older brother does not usually share his inner thoughts and experiences with his sister until they reach a certain level of maturity. Thanks to his trust and willingness to openly express his feelings, the work on the book moved along effectively and with joy––until it didn't. The first Friday in June 1999 we submitted a book proposal to a New York publishing company. When Sandy did not respond to our weekly Sunday check-ins, friends and family discovered he had suffered a second heart attack and his desire to conquer personal and societal mountain peaks had come to an end.

Many people who knew about the book project encouraged me to push through to finish the book without him. However, they had no concept of the concussive effect Sandy's death had on me and our family. Our ears were ringing, our minds were reeling, and our hearts were broken. The Stephens family meteor had burned out. My tears fell at the recorded sound of Sandy's voice, reading his narrative was painful, and interpreting his experiences for others, authentically, seemed impossible. It took more years than I expected to rise above my sadness and start reframing the manuscript.

A Walk with the Black Moses: Sandy Stephens' Inspiring Stories of Hope and Determination — is not the book Sandy expected to write and publish. Instead of being his autobiography, it is a representation of how his example to others regarding belief in self, goal setting with God's guidance, and hard work can result in a richly rewarding life and legacy. I believed the best way to find evidence of Sandy's impact on others was to send out a survey of seven open-ended questions and a comments page to a representative group of people. The survey questions can be found in Appendix A. Twenty-nine people, including family members, friends, teammates, fans, and colleagues responded to the survey. The observations of these supporters represent a snapshot of the influence Sandy had on the lives and aspirations of others. Their invaluable perceptions of how he walked through life and the legacy he left behind are shared throughout the book.

Intersecting with the receipt of the survey statements were historically significant events that affected me and my work. One such event shone bright for Americans and the world when Senator Barack Obama was nominated by a major party and elected the first Black President of the United States in 2008. President Obama stood on the shoulders of Frederick Douglass, who ran for president in 1848, prior to Black suffrage in the United States. Sandy's aspiration to become one of a small number of Black quarterbacks to lead a Division I college football team to national prominence paled in comparison to President Barack Obama's rise to the pinnacle of United States political heights. Sandy would have appreciated President Obama's election on many levels, but particularly because it gave credibility to Sandy's deeply ingrained belief that a Black man can accomplish any goal he faces when given an equal opportunity to compete.

Sandy always expected the best outcome for his efforts, and he was determined to reach unimpeachable acclaim as a professional Black quarterback in a society where such a goal was not expected or modeled for him. There is no question that he was a spark that ignited the prominence of Black quarterbacks on a national collegiate level. As the first Black Consensus All-American quarterback, Sandy became a model of opportunity for others who were watching. Some reactions to his success follow:

> Sandy's determination not to be denied the opportunity to display his athletic skills at the quarterback position spoke volumes about his tenacity. (O. Courtney––MN Brother-Friend)

> Sandy would be elated to know that the world is still talking about his abilities . . . and the opportunities he fought so hard for have opened to so many deserving young men. (C. Attaway (deceased)––Cousin)

Black quarterbacks are recognized and valued in college and professional football today. Before Sanford, they had little opportunity and respect. (J. Gloster––Daughter)

A Walk with the Black Moses: Sandy Stephens' Inspiring Stories of Hope and Determination — was chosen for the title of the book because of Sandy's feelings about their similarities. Moses and Sandy were leaders who believed they were destined to guide others to a "promised land." God's calling of the biblical Moses to be His messenger best exemplifies the fact that you do not have to be perfect to fulfill God's purpose for your life. Moses was not a perfect man, but he believed in and obeyed God's word. The life Sandy led was also imperfect but he remained driven by his belief in a spiritual purpose for his journey. He believed God chose him to set an example for others. The roads Sandy and Moses traveled in pursuit of obedience to God's plan for their lives were full of peaks and valleys and twists and turns. Each man endured the slings and arrows of defeat and basked in the praise and adoration of triumph. Neither Sandy nor Moses would dwell in the "promised land" of his dreams, but those who knew them and generations who followed their lead were influenced by the faith, perseverance, resilience, confidence, honesty, and hope they embodied.

This is the story of a Black individual, his life, loves, disappointments, and victories in an attempt to climb his Everest to promote the integrity of his race and to serve as an example to the great nation of the United States in regard to the humanity and bond of love and excellence among athletes whose careers should not be denied through prejudice or inopportunity to any American. **Sandy Stephens**

Sandy always wanted to deliver a message of encouragement. Other people, particularly his peers and other athletes, recognized his positive attitude and the example he set. He wanted the best for others so he encouraged his circle of family members and friends to take advantage of every opportunity they had to reach for and live their most dreamed-of existence. One example of his ability to inspire people to reach for the stars is noted by the following comment:

Sandy left his mark on everyone he ever met. That is the kind of person he was. He was certainly an inspiration to me and all the young guys who hung out on the corner at East End. We were fortunate to grow up at a time to witness his greatness. He will always be remembered as our hero in a small town in PA––Uniontown (C. Thomas––Extended Family)

As one of his devoted younger sisters, I felt compelled to follow Sandy's example to seek my most accomplished self and finish what we had started. Despite my personal grief, I was faced with societal and political disruptions in the United States that signaled the urgent need to share Sandy's personal journey with present and future generations. Clearly, positive role models and beacons of hope like Sandy Stephens are needed to help everyone, particularly our youth, direct their energy toward outlets that can bring lasting positive changes to their lives. The following testimonials show how his example was influential:

I remember going to the barbershop as a youngster and seeing Sandy's poster hanging from the wall and dreaming that mine might be there someday. (R. Bell––Extended Family)

Sandy was our living (non-fictional) sports hero growing up in Uniontown, PA, in the late 1950s. (G. Huey––Friend/Legacy Supporter)

I was a fan of Sandy Stephens and observed him from afar. I was much younger, but while growing up in Minneapolis, his presence at the university was larger than life for a junior high school kid. (B. Mchie––Fan/Historian)

He was there to counsel all the young athletes that were wanting to make their mark. He let them know it was attainable. (L. Hudson (deceased)––Gopher & NBA Athlete/Friend)

These comments were contributed by mature men, but the sense of hope they express was embedded in their spirits as youngsters. The youthful hope that Sandy's presence inspired in others is desperately needed today. It is not easy living in current times, despite electronic advancements—–and often because of them. We are losing a generation of children of color, particularly Black youth, to gun violence; unpunished police brutality; gentrification of neighborhoods that contributes to the loss of community; young people finding it easier to engage in negative outlets for their energy rather than hope for a future; the lack of enriching, affordable programs to keep youth engaged; and too many sources of misinformation. The challenge we face is seeking ways to remedy or transform these issues.

I turned to the survey responses for inspiration. The positive opinions expressed by the supporters lifted my heart and brightened my disposition. The time had come to speak for change by sharing a glimpse of Sandy's life experiences and how he felt about winning, losing, and persevering.

The goal of *A Walk with the Black Moses: Sandy Stephens' Inspiring Stories of Hope and Determination* — is to bring the reader enlightenment of the mind, understanding of the heart, and enrichment of the spirit. Evaluate your internal barometer as you read. Are there dreams and passions you want to explore? Why have you been too timid to pursue them? Is fear of failure getting in your way? Your personal **greatness** may be waiting for you to begin the climb toward it. The journey starts with belief in self, setting lofty goals, never losing sight of your envisioned success, and having the determination to persist against all odds.

Let's take a walk with the Black Moses, Sandy Stephens, to find out what motivated him and the principles he maintained in his quest to build an athletic and personal legacy of greatness.

SANDY STEPHENS
1997 ROSE BOWL HALL OF FAME

'62 MVP ROSE BOWL
'61 ALL AMERICAN QB

Chapter 1

BEING STEPHENS

ANCESTRY

A line of descent: lineage; especially honorable, noble, or aristocratic descent. (https://www.merriam-webster.com)

GEORGIA––PATERNAL ROOTS

Sandy and I were born into a family of ancestral strength and courage. The shining paternal examples of early fortitude were our great-grandparents, Jack (man), the descriptor written on his bill of sale, and Victoria, the product of a union between a slave woman and a plantation owner whose names are unknown to us. Slaves were stripped of their African family names as part of their bondage in the United States. Macon, Georgia, municipal records show that Jack chose Thomas as a surname. He and Victoria lived through and were manumitted from slavery. As freed people they married and built their home on land deeded to them by Victoria's father.

Jack and Victoria Thomas were industrious, loving people who reared ten children. One of those children was our grandmother, Rosa. Rosa fell in love with a former slave from a nearby plantation called George. After his freedom and before his marriage, George assumed the surname Stephens. The spelling of the name appears several different ways in census records, but we have always used Stephens as our preferred spelling. Rosa and George had two children, Sanford Emory (Dad) and Frances Alma (Aunt Alma).

I do not know the family dynamic or the number of individuals who lived in the homestead, but Aunt Alma told me that when our grandparents separated, Grandpa George wanted to take Dad with him.

The family objected because they did not believe Grandpa George would be able to support his son. The story of Grandpa George's life after leaving the family is unknown since none of the elders interviewed remembered hearing anyone refer to him again. Dad's life was profoundly changed by the absence of his father.

Now single, Rosa and her children lived with her mother and father until Rosa's untimely death when her children were minors. Dad and Aunt Alma were split up and sent to live with the families of two of Rosa's brothers. Aunt Alma joined a family headed by a loving uncle and his wife in a comfortable home in Savannah, Georgia. Dad was not as fortunate. Reliable family members recalled that Dad's uncle physically mistreated him. (Years later, Dad had violent nightmares. We never talked about why, but I often wonder if he was reliving the horrors of his childhood.) After a particularly brutal beating, Dad knew his temperament, strength, and youthful pride would not allow him to continue being a punching bag for the man. He was reared to be respectful to his elders, but he was on the verge of fighting back. He prayed for deliverance and when he appealed to a different uncle and aunt for shelter, his prayers were answered.

Dad was welcomed into his new surroundings with love. Many years later, our oldest living cousin told us her parents bought Dad a suit and a "good" pair of shoes, so he would be presentable for high school graduation. Graduation was a precious first step toward Dad's goal of becoming a doctor. He resolved to work toward that goal no matter what challenges he faced. Unfortunately, the financial wherewithal required for him to gain his degree as a doctor was insurmountable. He could not work enough jobs to stockpile the amount of funding needed. Always a man with a plan, Dad changed course and decided to channel his intellect and efforts in pursuit of the closely aligned, but different vocation––mortician.

PENNSYLVANIA—DAD

Another uncle, Sanford Milton Thomas, a no-nonsense, retired soldier who had served in the Spanish-American War, invited his young namesake to come to Pittsburgh to live with him and his wife, Viola. Uncle Sanford supported his nephew's dream of becoming a mortician. Dad had been working multiple jobs while attending Ballard Normal School, a combined primary and secondary school for the freedmen in Macon. He was encouraged by Uncle Sanford's invitation. Dad knew that by moving to Pittsburgh and with the love of his surrogate parents, Uncle Sanford and Aunt Vi, he would have family encouragement, financial support, and the ability to further his education at a faster pace.

Dad continued to work multiple jobs in Pittsburgh to become solvent enough to continue his education. He was a skilled construction laborer, clothes presser, glazier, pullman porter, and insurance salesman. (Household maintenance and repair skills were passed on to me by my dad thanks to his breadth of experience and willingness to share his expertise. His tutelage helped me to become a homeowner who can troubleshoot most household situations.) All Dad's hard work paid off. He was able to move to New York, attend Renouard School of Embalming, and graduate with his embalmer certification. The convictions and strength of character Dad exhibited in pursuit of his goals help to inform the reader about factors that predisposed Sandy to become a man with high self-esteem, a strong work ethic, and a determination to succeed.

PENNSYLVANIA—MATERNAL ROOTS

Unfortunately, we do not have as much information about our maternal great-grandparents but we know they were based in Pittsburgh,

PA. Our maternal Great-Grandmother Julia (born Juliet as a twin to Romeo), was very influential in Mom's life. We know from ancestry search records that her husband's name was John Ridgley. Information about John Ridgley was recently discovered by another family member but his name was not mentioned in conversation when my brothers, sister, and I were young. Mom and other family members shared pictures of Great-Grandma Julia. Our Grandmother Bessie looked like a kinder, gentler version of her mother.

Sandy and I had a loving, joyful, and deeply rooted relationship with our maternal grandparents, Berkley (PapPap) and Bessie (NanNan) Pryor. Our adoration of them is based on their presence in our lives. Making the trip to their home in Pittsburgh always caused a heightened sense of anticipation. Summer-long trips for me were to attend Vacation Bible School. Sandy had comfortable lodging when he had a summer job as a steelworker. NanNan and PapPap hosted celebrations ranging from family birthdays, anniversaries, weddings, holidays, and home goings. They exuded warmth, laughter, spirituality, and discipline. Their home held a special place in our youthful and young adult memories. We laughed, we played, we were nourished intellectually and spiritually, we were loved unconditionally, and we learned to be respectful.

When we were very young, Sandy and I had great fun with our cousins who lived with our grandparents. It was joyful running up the stairs in the front hall, across the landing, down the adjoining back stairs into the kitchen, through the kitchen's hall door, and back again. Naturally, we made the circuit as often as we could until the first adult reprimand came. Always resourceful, we switched to sliding down the banister of the front stairs. The banister in Pittsburgh didn't have a knob on the newel post, which made it easy to slide down and dismount without stopping. (The banister at home had a knob which required stopping with skill to avoid pain at the end of the slide.) All the running and sliding brought shouts of STOP IT!! from the adults in the household at a decibel level that required no interpretation. We learned to find other quieter ways to entertain ourselves until being called to set the table for the family meal.

Just as at home, children were responsible for setting up and clearing the table, then washing and drying the dishes. Afterward, we were free to return to whatever activities were dictated by the season. Since most of the prolonged time we spent in Pittsburgh occurred in the summer, the preferred option was to go outside to enjoy riding bikes, roller skating, playing hide 'n' seek, and other neighborhood adventures. If it was dark outside when we finished our chores, we spent time playing board and card games, dominoes, jacks, pick-up-sticks, and more with NanNan and Aunt Betty, Mom's younger sister. Aunt Betty was the jacks champion. She showed no mercy, which helped our expertise. It was hard for my friends to beat me when I returned home from visits to Pittsburgh and Aunt Betty's expert training about how to win.

While we kids were entertaining ourselves, PapPap was usually listening to the radio—baseball games were his passion, tending to the fish in his sizable aquarium, or tinkering with his train sets. He often retired to the quiet solitude of his room, where he waited to give all of us a foot-tickling, rib-splitting session before we went to bed. PapPap worked with his hands most of his life which left him with a grip strong enough to overcome the most frantic attempts to escape his grasp. Looking back, I believe it was a way for our grandparents to use up any remaining energy in our small bodies. Washing up, brushing teeth, and saying our prayers rounded out a day's happiness.

Thankfully we spent enough years with our grandparents to soak up their essential ways of being. They always reinforced our parents' teachings about the importance of conducting ourselves with dignity and pride. They modeled love of God, hard work, educational thirst, perseverance, and a sense of humor. The memory of NanNan sitting in her chair reading her Bible and PapPap in his room smoking his pipe while reading a favorite paperback will forever conjure up warm emotions.

PENNSYLVANIA—MOM

We did not know in our youth how much NanNan contributed to Mom's musical genius and her grandchildren's musical gifts. Mom expanded her unassailable belief in living a Christian life when, as a young woman, she followed in NanNan's organist footsteps in the music ministry of Bidwell Street Presbyterian Church. Mom's exceptional musical talent and work ethic helped her earn enough money to attend Fisk University in Nashville, Tennessee, several years after high school graduation.

Helen Pryor immersed herself fully in campus life. She debated about whether to major in chemistry or music but decided to pursue a career in music. She became a protégé of John W. Work, renowned composer and a director of the famed Fisk Jubilee Singers. Mom spoke glowingly about how much she appreciated being mentored by Dr. Work. I recognized their mutual admiration when Dr. and Mrs. Work hosted our stay at Fisk for the twenty-fifth anniversary of Mom's graduating class. I was sixteen years old and profoundly moved when I realized my mother was a respected friend of celebrated men such as American historian, John Hope Franklin, and physicist, James Raymond Lawson. Listening to them reminisce about the times they enjoyed during their college days helped to bring life to the scrapbook photos Mom had shared with us. They showed her gathering with friends outside Jubilee Hall and other campus landmarks, enjoying the beach, attending Alpha Kappa Alpha (AKA) sorority events, and singing with the Fisk Women's Chorus. It was a wonderful time in her life.

In June 1935 Mom graduated from Fisk University *cum laude* with a Bachelor of Arts degree, with a major in Music––Piano and Organ. After graduation, Mom spent a short time teaching at a small North Carolina school. She was not permitted to teach music and her net monthly salary was less than $40. Naturally she did not hesitate to accept an offer to teach music at Florida Agricultural & Mechanical College (FAMC) (now FAMU) in Tallahassee, Florida. The pay was better; she felt confident she could build a career as a piano, organ, and voice teacher; and she could interact with her AKA sorors. Mom was also given the opportunity to serve as the director of the Women's Glee Club which received acclaim under her guidance. Once more Mom was very happy with her life on a college campus. She was a favorite of her students, pupils, colleagues, and friends. However, her trip back to Pittsburgh for summer vacation in 1939 proved to be life altering.

PENNSYLVANIA––MOM and DAD

Our mother and father brought their values, virtues, talents, and gifts to their relationship when they were introduced by a mutual friend on a Pittsburgh tennis court during her summer break from teaching. Dad was impressed with Mom's athleticism on the court when she kept pace with his considerable tennis skills by hitting him in the mid-section with a tennis ball. They both admitted Dad won that original tennis match, but their tennis matches continued to be hotly contested. Once they spent time together off the court, the couple realized they were also compatible spiritually, intellectually, artistically, and emotionally. Mom returned to Florida after the break and Dad remained in Pittsburgh to complete both his apprenticeship as a mortician at a funeral home and his licensure as a master embalmer. The obstacle standing in their way was distance. They lived in separate cities, miles apart.

Despite the distance between them their love grew and after many letters and long-distance calls, Dad convinced Mom to return to Pittsburgh to marry him. They wed in November 1939. According to an article in the *Pittsburgh Courier*, the Stephens wedding was the city's social event of the fall season. After their marriage, the couple bought a three-story duplex in Uniontown, Pennsylvania, which they converted into a family residence and funeral business.

PENNSYLVANIA—STEPHENS FAMILY

In early 1940, Mom and Dad opened the Stephens Funeral Home. It became one of two Black funeral homes within a block of each other in the

East End of town. Despite the close competition, the business flourished, and the family grew to include a son (Sanford II), a daughter (Barbara), and twins (Raymond and Joyce). We lived on the second floor of the building above the chapel, music room, office, and casket room on the first floor. The garage, in-take room, furnace/work bench, fuel storage room, and morgue occupied the basement.

We grew up in an era when children were truthfully raised by the village. Love, support, social consciousness, life lessons, cautions, and discipline were meted out by whichever adult was closest to the situation. Elders such as Miss Liza, Aunt Me and other adults in the community had the implied permission from our parents to correct any of our inappropriate behavior, if warranted. Correction back then translated to verbal or physical reprimand. I have no memory of anyone other than our parents spanking me, but Miss Liza shared a story about giving a young Sandy the choice of going back outside to face down a bully who was threatening him or returning home to her punishment for not standing up for himself. Sandy chose dealing with the bully.

As children of Sanford and Helen Stephens we were known by everyone, and we were painfully aware of how many eyes could be watching us at any given moment. Such awareness probably kept us from trying too many ventures that we knew would not be approved by Dad and Mom. Although Sandy is included in that statement, the truth is that my resistance to being disciplined kept me from participating in most stupid pranks suggested by my peers. I cannot speak for Sandy. The societal norms for what boys could and girls could not get away with was weighted heavily in favor of boys. Consequently, Sandy had a wider range of territory he could explore and experiences he could enjoy out of the sight of prying adult eyes. The back yard and neighborhood were my base and I could always find something to entertain myself with close to home.

Home for us was complicated. Most of the time we could come and go with ease. If we were not doing homework, chores, or being productive in some other way, sitting around the house was not expected or encouraged. I had places where I could hide to read my books in peace and quiet but we had mature apple trees in the backyard that became some of my favorite perches. Climbing trees, roller skating up and down the sidewalk, enjoying the family swing set, and playing with friends in the neighborhood were my usual activities. When I finally gained permission to go across the street to the playground or to ride my bicycle my world grew.

Sandy's world was expansive because he was involved in sports that covered the year. He could be found on a baseball field, at track practice, on a football field, in a gymnasium, or on the playground playing basketball throughout the seasons. He also explored different parts of the East End on his bicycle. One incident Mom recounted occurred when she was sitting on the porch of a friend who lived several blocks away from the house. They looked across an open lot and saw a bicycle rolling along with a youngster standing on his head on the seat. Mom gasped at the sight and wondered who in the world the rider could be. Her friend calmly told her it was Sandy. They watched as he skillfully flipped back onto the seat and proceeded to continue his ride. I do not know what the conversation was between them later, but I can imagine Mom used more than her usual few words to express her displeasure.

Neither Sandy nor I, and later the twins, found any comfort in Mom's displeasure. A look of disappointment from her was as soul searing as Dad's belt was physically painful. When Sandy and I were youngsters, we were particularly uncomfortable with the *don't walk, don't talk* restrictions imposed on us when a funeral service was being conducted in the chapel below our living quarters. Any sound or activity we made could be detected by the grieving family and funeral attendees. Such a disturbance was considered disrespectful and punishment worthy. We tried to exit the premises well ahead of the time for the funeral but occasionally we did not act soon enough. In those instances, Sandy was not afraid to take steps to free us from enduring the *quiet zone* mandate. I was pleased when he included me in whatever escape plan he had devised. The scene could play out something like this:

"Hey, Barb, the music is starting for the funeral downstairs. We need to get out of here quick! We can't go down the front stairs because the pallbearers are sitting in the hallway outside the doors to the chapel. Plus, Daddy will see us if we go that way. Come on, hurry up!" Sandy whispered hoarsely. "Let's go down the back stairs, through the public bathroom, the office, the casket room, then out the side door to the yard. Daddy is busy with the family of the deceased and Mommy is playing the piano for the service. They won't notice." Stealthily, we carried out Sandy's plan, escaped the anguish of Dad's clients, and made it to freedom.

No doubt our parents knew what we were doing since they both had acute hearing, but they let us work our plan without censure.

In 1958 our family dynamic changed. Before Sandy left for college our grandparents moved from their roots in Pittsburgh to a house in Uniontown. A level of jealousy had existed toward our cousins because all their lives they had lived with NanNan and PapPap and they shared a level of closeness with which we could not identify. Finally, we could enjoy being with our grandparents daily. (One time I "ran away" from home as far as their house across town——it lasted one afternoon!)

Our grandparents' change of address did not last long. NanNan suffered from and succumbed to a massive stroke early in 1959. She was an extraordinary woman who made an indelible imprint on our lives. Ironically, the day of her death, Mom and Dad were visiting Sandy in Minnesota to see him play in one of his first collegiate varsity games against the U. of Michigan Wolverines. Although Mom, Dad, and Sandy were devastated when they heard the news about NanNan, they knew my training in funeral home procedures guaranteed that PapPap would be supported and NanNan's remains would be handled with love and care.

After NanNan's passing, PapPap moved in with us. The space in the house that had served over the years as a casket room, playroom, and storage was converted into a bedroom to accommodate the transition. Those were special times, especially for our brother Raymond, who shared a bedroom with PapPap. Ray could probably write a book about their talks and the wisdom shared between them as roommates.

PENNSYLVANIA——MUSIC

Funerals mandated silence, but that was not the usual atmosphere in our home. Juxtaposed with elements of life and death, our home resounded with music most of the time. Mom could be found in the music room coaching a vocalist preparing for a performance, giving piano lessons to young students, or playing the piano for her own enjoyment. None of us could play the piano as well as Mom, but we all love music and sing admirably. We sang while cleaning up the kitchen after dinner, at family sing-alongs in the music room, along with the songs on the record player, mimicking the *Hit Parade* artists on the radio, and eventually belting out tunes from television programs. We chose songs enjoyed by both generations when we sang to overcome the tedium of the 50-mile trip to Pittsburgh. Dad often led the family chorus with his rich baritone voice. I remember Ketty Lester's "Love Letters" being a favorite for harmonizing on the road trips.

We particularly enjoyed singing the songs Cousin Cat taught us. She and Mom shared strong Negro spiritual and gospel music backgrounds. Many of the songs we sang sparked a sense of ancestral recognition in our souls. We were unaware at the time that Cousin Cat and Mom were helping us experience the rich musical heritage we were gifted with from both the Ridgley/Pryor and Thomas/Stephens sides of our family tree. Music was indeed an integral part of our being and so was dancing.

Assuming the sibling leadership role was the norm for Sandy. I was second in the sibling line and expected to follow his lead in most instances. Therefore, it was a lot of fun when Sandy came home for college break and we switched roles. Minnesota was not considered a hot spot for the latest rock and roll or rhythm and blues tunes or dance moves, so he was at a disadvantage. He depended on me to bring him up to speed on the latest hits and dance steps. Finally, I was able to lead him and I loved it.

The Lafayette JHS Youth Center (the Center) was our spot from age 12 to 16 for recreation and dancing every Saturday night during the school year. As a member of the organizing committee, I had a stockpile of 45 rpm records that included all the latest songs on the music charts. Also, friends returning home from D.C., New York, Detroit, Chicago, and other music meccas brought the latest dance moves with them.

Armed with these resources, Sandy and I practiced the slop, mashed potatoes, funky chicken, and other popular dances of the time to get Sandy ready to strut his stuff on the dance floor at the Ivory Ballroom (the Ivory). The Ivory was our dance outlet when we reached age 16 and outgrew the Center. Pittsburgh radio personalities brought national recording artists to the Ivory and the dances attracted youth from cities, towns, and hamlets between Uniontown and Pittsburgh. I was not old enough to attend with

Sandy during his first visits home from college, but I knew everyone was waiting to see the hometown hero perform. Thanks to our sessions, Sandy did not disappoint. He continued to be one of the sharpest dressed, smoothest dancers on the floor.

It is hard for some people to imagine, but we had parties in our home. Sandy was at the University of Minnesota by the time the twins and I had parties in the chapel, but he was quoted once as being a music fan with the ambition to be a disc jockey (DJ). The quote tickled me because a DJ contest at the Center resulted in a win for me. The DJ talents came in handy when we gathered in the chapel with our friends for a party. The chapel was spacious, it had a tile floor, and we were away from our living area. If we assured the group ahead of time that Dad did not have a person's body in the morgue, everyone relaxed and we were able to dance, sing, and have a good time. We could put the record player on the piano in the music room, spin LPs and 45s, and be amazed as brother Ray played by ear songs such as "Fingertips" by Little Stevie Wonder. The song was one of Ray's favorites and a crowd pleaser. We were grateful to Dad for allowing us to use the space for our teenage fun. Many memories, adventures, and stories are embedded in the walls of that majestic home. They run the gamut from hope and laughter to despair and tears.

We were blessed with a childhood filled with the role modeling and teaching of loving parents. We were gifted at birth with intelligence, athleticism, musical talent, and personality. Building on that base, Dad and Mom imbued our beings with faith, a moral compass, a strong work ethic, educational zeal, self-esteem, pride, and dignity. As we matured, common sense, business acumen, and service to others were added to our competencies.

Putting these attributes and other parental guidance into practice became innate. Sandy used all the principles in his belief system to gain a life of personal satisfaction and public recognition. He had high expectations for himself and for the people in his sphere of influence. Including the familial and physical background of Sandy's upbringing is important to understand the elements that contributed to the ways he faced various situations.

The STEPHENS Family 1952

FAITH

To have faith is to be sure of the things we hope for, to be certain of the things we cannot see. Hebrews 11:1 (NIV Bible)

PENNSYLVANIA––DEVELOPMENT

We grew up in a faith-based family bolstered by the African Methodist Episcopal (AME) family background of our dad; the Presbyterian principles that embrace generosity, social justice, education, and baptism exhibited by NanNan and Mom; and eventually the teachings and effects of Baptist doctrine and practices on our minds and spirits. We were taught belief in the Holy Trinity, the power of prayer, the importance of having a moral compass, and how to strive to be Christ-like in our interactions with and compassion for others. Such beliefs provided the underpinning for our faith-based actions girded by Biblical guidance:

> Have I not commanded you? Be strong and courageous. Do not be terrified, do not be discouraged, for the LORD your god will be with you wherever you go. Joshua 1:9 (NIV Bible)

> Trust in the LORD with all your heart and lean not on your own understanding; in all your ways acknowledge him, and he will make your paths straight.
> Proverbs 3:5-6 (NIV Bible)

One close friend expressed how Sandy's belief system impacted his life:

> There were life lessons that I learned from Sandy that I will never forget, not the least of which is helping me to discover what it means to have a personal relationship with Jesus Christ.
> (O. Courtney––MN Brother-Friend)

Although attending church and/or Sunday School each week was a Stephens family mandate, we have lived a fascinating spiritual journey. As children we were christened at the Bidwell Street Presbyterian church in

Pittsburgh. In Uniontown, Sandy and I spent our youth participating in the choir and other activities at Zion A.M.E. (African Methodist Episcopal) church where Mom was one of the musicians. She was sharing her musical and choral talents with the Zion A.M.E. congregation because her contribution was welcomed and appreciated. Mom did not receive the same attitude when she attended a service at the Presbyterian church in downtown Uniontown. That congregation did not take the time to find out what a brilliant musician they had in their sanctuary. They simply regarded Mom as a Black woman who was not welcome to share a pew with them. Their disdain was painful since Mom had been a devout Presbyterian her entire life. This was not the type of Christianity she had been taught. I always felt the group's attitude was more their loss than Mom's. They missed out on enjoying the artistry of Helen Pryor Stephens on their impressive pipe organ. She would have made it sing.

By the time Dad decided to join the Baptist church, Mom was balancing getting four children ready for Sunday School and/or church and preparing the Sunday meal. She did not become a member but she enthusiastically endorsed the four of us being baptized at Mt. Rose Baptist Church. Sandy was moved to join the church during a visit home from college. Mom and Dad were overjoyed that he was giving his life to Christ.

We have joined other churches since leaving Uniontown but Mt. Rose remains our home church.

No matter what denomination we joined, the no church attendance, no outdoor time in the fall and winter and no playground freedom in the summer never wavered. Playground deprivation was painful because it was central to our summer fun. It really was not necessary to direct us to attend Sunday School––because it was such a constant part of our lives but also because we thoroughly enjoyed it.

By the time we reached high school, Sunday School at our church was an extension of our education in actual ways. Our Sunday School teacher, the late Mrs. Nancy Jenkins, was also the playground director. We considered her a surrogate parent. Consequently, she was able to bring the Bible to life for us and make the lessons relatable to our teenage world. "Miss" Jenkins, the term of endearment we used for her, gave us unconditional love. She had high expectations for our behavior which helped many of us avoid teenage unpleasantness. She and Sandy were particularly close. Both of us appreciated her love and respected her tutelage and mentoring.

Along with moral and ethical teachings, and the examples of the adults in our family and community, the Stephens children were imbued, body and soul, with an unwavering belief in our God-given gifts and talents. However, when Sandy was a teenage athletic star who seemed to be impressed with his own press, Mom reminded him that everything he had accomplished was made possible through the grace and mercy of his Lord and Savior Jesus Christ, not Sandy Stephens. Sandy took her reminder to heart and tried not to lose sight of the meaning of her words as his career and reputation gained renown. His self-esteem and swagger did not diminish, but in the future, he was careful not to forget the source of his strength.

MINNESOTA––EXPLORATION

Sandy questioned the why and how of things throughout his youth. He was driven to become a life-long seeker of knowledge about the mysteries of the Universe, God, and his purpose on earth. He was surrounded by people of faith who espoused the power and guidance found in Biblical teachings and he wanted to understand it all on a higher plane. In that spirit, as Sandy studied, his favorite college courses were psychology and philosophy——both of which explore the workings of the mind. Most of his life was centered on athletics and he became intrigued by comparisons and contrasts between athletics and life as he studied. In a philosophy paper entitled "Crisis vs. Choice," Sandy explained how the difference between making a conscious choice, rather than reacting to a crisis, is the best approach to making good decisions on and off the field of play:

Throughout a person's life many crises occur that require a choice of action or decision . . . When an individual has a true God relationship, he cares for God, himself, and other individuals. But the pains of choice and crisis even after a relationship with God are not easy and no one is promised an easier time.

Athletics serve as a practice field for everyday living. Two slogans that can be found on some locker room walls were always appealing to me, although it took more than reading them to fully appreciate their real value in football and in life. The first stated, "Ingredients of a Successful Player: 95% mental attitude, 4% other factors, and 1% ability." The second stated, "When the one great scorer comes to write against your name, he asks not who won, but how well you played the game."

Slogans such as these help to propel an individual who knows, in crisis or choice situations, all that can be asked of one is for one to do the best he can whatever the outcome may be. The earnestness and energy applied to the situation are the primary factors viewed to be most important. And if one has faith in God, the individual acquires the needed strength to persevere in athletics or any other facet of life, including crisis or fear.

When the <u>request</u> is not right——God says, "No!"
When the <u>time</u> is not right——God says, "Slow!"
When <u>we</u> are not right——God says, "Grow!"
When <u>everything's</u> right——God says, "Go!"

Sandy Stephens

(cf. Bill Hybel's quote on izquotes.com)

Sandy was always willing to share his understanding of the parental and Biblical lessons we were taught. He was gifted with natural talent, intelligence, and charisma. A dear friend says it well in his comment:

> Sandy was a magnetic force. He believed in the real hearts of all people. Sandy was a real person who gave back to life and wanted nothing in return except respect as a human being. Sandy was a giant among people and lived his faith and heart for and to all those he came in touch with. (T. Hitchcock–– Marathoner/Writer/Friend)

EDUCATION

Education is the process of facilitating learning or the acquisition of knowledge, skills, values, beliefs, and habits.
(https//en.m.wikipedia.org)

Mom and Dad held education as the means to a better existence. They were intelligent individuals who had a thirst for knowledge and the passionate desire to rise above their circumstances through hard work. Dad satisfied his educational goal when he became a master embalmer and established his own funeral home business. Mom fulfilled her dream of sharing music with others by completing her degree, directing choirs, and teaching individual performers. Together they provided excellent examples of how to set goals, work hard to reach personal success, and learn how to share our gifts and talents with others in the community. Sandy and I were the first recipients of our parents' steadfast belief that, after our faith, education should be the most important emphasis in our lives.

PENNSYLVANIA––EXPECTATIONS

Sandy was my larger-than-life hero as a child. We were inseparable playmates until he started first grade. Kindergarten was not offered on our side of Uniontown in 1946 and Mom did not see an advantage for us to attend a school out of our neighborhood. She was a capable teacher who gave us excellent pre-school preparation, but I was impatient to go to the **real** school. After an agonizing two years of waiting to reach the age of six years old, I was ready to join Sandy as he crossed the street to enter the doors of the place of my dreams––the majestic beige brick building with the pillars, East End Elementary School. Excitement is an inadequate word to use for my feelings. Sandy and I would be in school together now. It was a special time.

School attendance was not optional or merely desired. Illness was the only excuse our parents accepted for absence from school. If we were too sick to go to school, the doctor was called to the house. The usual remedy for most conditions back then was a shot of penicillin. Penicillin is a painful, stinging serum and the family doctor was a friend of our parents who had no bedside manner. Being threatened with his arrival and treatment was incentive enough to keep us from faking an illness. Faking never crossed our minds, but prior to my turn to attend school, Sandy came home with the measles and chicken pox. Mom's caution for me to stay away from him so I would not get infected was futile. I could not let him suffer alone. Consequently, Sandy and I shared the conditions simultaneously and I was free to go to school without missing time for contracting those diseases. Happily, we were not sick very often and the doctor's capable, but unfriendly attention was rarely needed.

Sandy and I occasionally shared disciplinary action, but one punishment Sandy and I could not share was losing athletic opportunities or awards due to earning a C in a subject—I did not participate in any extracurricular sports. Our parents believed a C student had no time for non-academic activities since those hours needed to be used to study and improve grade levels. Sandy recalls how he learned the hard way the consequence of disregarding the academic mandate imposed by our parents:

> Basketball began in 5th grade with the grade school leagues in Uniontown. In 7th grade I made the Junior High traveling team along with a friend. My dad had me kicked off the team because I had two Cs on my report card. He also took my championship jacket from me and gave it to another player. These actions were a definite wake up call to let me know how serious my dad was about academics. He said that, being a minority, I had to be twice as good in my academic work to be given any consideration against my competition in all endeavors.

For me, not adhering to the no-C grade rule could mean being stuck in the house for six weeks waiting for the next reporting period to end. For Sandy, it meant sitting on the bench or not being able to participate in the sport he was playing at the time—baseball, football, basketball, or track. Therefore, we put in the work to earn As and Bs in all academic subjects for a personal sense of pride and with those parental sanctions in mind.

When we were in elementary and junior high school we were graded on class effort and citizenship also. Our parents expected us to give 100% effort at all times, in class or out. Not earning an A grade in effort and citizenship was tantamount to failing in an academic subject. In the opinion of our parents, when we performed at a high level of competence and exhibited good citizenship, we were positive reflections of our family.

Sandy and I carried forward the beliefs instilled in us regarding academic, athletic, and personal practice. Wisely, we surrounded ourselves with friends and family who supported us and who were influenced by our example per the comments below:

I think Sandy's influence on me was so great because there weren't many guys going to college. Blue collar was the message of the time (work). (C. Thomas–– Extended Family)

We were classmates and friends from 1st grade through 5th grade and then again from 9th grade through 12th grade. He (Sandy) was always a sharing & fun person to be with and he strived for excellence in every aspect of life. I kept all the clippings and talked to several *People* magazine people about his achievements. (C. Wilson––Uniontown Friend/Fan)

Sandy was a very bright well-read guy who could engage in any conversation or topic that was on the table at the time. (M. Harrison––Friend/Program Director)

[He set a] good example for youth and articulateness. (A. Hjelm––Fan/Gopher Cheerleader)

MINNESOTA––COMPLETION

Despite our parents' emphasis on education and the pursuit of post-secondary credentials, it took considerable time for Sandy and me to complete our bachelor's degrees. Both of us spent years working, rearing children, and encouraging other family members to keep pursuing their educational goals while deferring our own studies.

My post-secondary educational journey began in 1961 at The Pennsylvania State University (Penn State). In 1963 I left college and went to work in the nation's capital. School was the furthest thing from my mind. After my arrival in Minnesota I continued my pursuit of a baccalaureate degree through the Regents Scholarship program that was available to University civil service workers. My family and job responsibilities left enough time for me to take one class at a time. I completed the requirements for the Associate in Arts (A.A.) degree––90 credits and passing the comprehensive exam––on the way to my final goal. Mom cried when I left Penn State, but I promised her I would finish my degree eventually.

I kept my promise when I participated in graduation after completion of the degree coursework. The remaining requirements for the Bachelor of General Studies degree were finished in 1990––29 years after my freshman year. Mom and Dad had passed away, but Sandy, Joyce, my children, niece, ex-husband, and close friends were there to witness the culmination of my dream.

From that time on, I encouraged Sandy to keep such an educational goal in mind for himself, no matter how long or difficult the journey up that mountain became. Somewhere on the path to pursuing his passions, dreams, and aspirations, Sandy had forgotten our dad's admonition to be better equipped than others to receive serious consideration for any opportunity. If a bachelor's degree is a required qualification for a position and a candidate does not have a degree, their application cannot be considered. There is no recourse. Sandy was denied entry into a pool for an athletic department job that was a perfect match for his background because he lacked a four-year post-secondary degree. The loss of that opportunity made him determined to take the steps necessary to keep such a denial from happening again.

University of Minnesota graduation was always Sandy's goal and what his heart yearned to accomplish. However, by the time he decided to complete his bachelor's degree, he discovered that the services offered by Metropolitan State University (Metro State) in St. Paul provided the means for him to complete his educational goals in a reasonable amount of time. By working closely with an advisor at Metro State, Sandy was able to combine his life experiences with academic coursework. His thirst for knowledge and excitement about being on a campus as a student gave him a renewed sense of scholastic purpose and determination. We shared a car at the time and his demeanor made me smile each time I dropped him off for class. The Sandy **strut** was back. He was excited, prepared, and ready to share his wisdom with fellow students.

One of the proudest moments of Sandy's adult life was celebrating his graduation in 1994––a few months prior to his 54th birthday and 35 years after his freshman year in college. It was a glorious day for all of us as we witnessed Sandy and his friend and teammate Carl Eller, proudly march down the aisle to receive their Bachelor of Arts degrees. Sandy had set another goal and conquered the mountain it symbolized. Sanford and Helen Stephens would be very proud of the way their four children persevered to reach educational goals that led to successful careers in business, education, and service.

ATHLETICISM

The quality of being coordinated and physically strong while also having stamina and coordination. (https://www.yourdictionary.com)

PENNSYLVANIA--SKILLS DEVELOPMENT

My brothers Sandy and Raymond (Ray) became the next generation of athletic stars in our family. We all inherited our parents' athleticism and competitive spirit, but the boys had the opportunity to show off their skills. Sandy's primary leadership role model and his first athletic hero was Dad. The initial impetus to excel and gain recognition as an athlete came to Sandy in the early 1950s when he was a pre-teen admiring Dad's tennis trophies and plaques on the wall in his office. Dad was a multiple-sport athlete who excelled in baseball and football in his youth and tennis as an adult. He recognized Sandy's athletic ability in the early stages of his development.

Sports were a focal point for everyone in Uniontown. We excelled at dodgeball, four squares, tetherball, and competitive basketball and volleyball games. On the east side of our small town, where the highest concentration of culturally diverse families existed during our time there, the connection between families was strong. The East End had two elementary schools and one junior high school. The west side had multiple elementary schools and one junior high school. Other high schools existed in the area but most students from both sides of town and up the mountain converged on Uniontown JSHS for their final three years.

East End playground, Lafayette Junior High School (JHS), and Uniontown Joint Senior High School (JSHS) were key venues in our youthful development. Many celebrated athletes who honed their skills on the courts, fields, gymnasiums, and stadiums of Southwestern Pennsylvania came out of Uniontown and the surrounding cities and towns. A high percentage of those heralded and heavily recruited athletes would have been young women if similar opportunities for them had existed but their era was yet to come.

The playground program in Uniontown was inaugurated in June of 1945 with nine sites. George Von Benko writes, "The crown jewel of the playground system's summer program was its highly competitive Senior Recreation Basketball League, which reached its heyday from 1959 to 1970." [1] (Von Benko 2012)

East End playground always entered strong teams and their biggest rivals were usually Lincoln View (West End) teams. Uniontown JSHS's basketball greats are mentioned in the article. East End players such as Sandy Stephens, Ray Stephens, John Moorman, Ray Parson, Don Yates, Pat Yates, Stu Lantz, and Ben Gregory sparred against Lincoln View stalwarts such as John Unice, Miles Cohen, Dave Marovich, Owen Silbaugh, and Jerry Meadows. League championship games drew hundreds of spectators. Several friends gave testament to the lifelong familial ties they developed with Sandy on playgrounds, in schools, and in our neighborhood:

> He (Sandy) was like a mentor and big brother to me (and Munce and Pars and Don, the list goes on and on). We had a special chemistry from the time we met on the buckets court as kids. . . . part of it was "cultural" as both our families owned their own businesses, our dads knew each other, and we were both minorities (him Black and me Jewish) from different parts of town. Sandy and I over the years used to always treat each other with this amazing dignity and respect. . . . (M. Cohen—— Uniontown Friend/Legacy Supporter)
>
> He always thought about his childhood friends. (C. McLee—— Uniontown Brother-Friend)
>
> His caring for those who lifted him on his way. (K. Finney (deceased)——Uniontown Brother-Friend)
>
> He was the best friend you could have. (M. Hickenbottom—— Lifelong Friend)
>
> Funny——always could make me laugh. One of the nicest people you will ever meet. (G. Bell——Friend/Former Brother-in-law)

Dad was able to talk to his eldest son from personal athletic experience about the type of attitude and preparation required if Sandy wanted to reach his goals. Most noteworthy, Dad tutored Sandy in where to place talent in the formula for elite athlete status. He posited that athletic talent is a critical component for success that becomes a powerful weapon when coupled with leadership, competitive fire, perseverance, determination, and teamwork. The total formula would make the difference between success and failure in his goal to reach elite athlete status.

Sandy shared Dad's love for baseball and competed in youth baseball leagues from childhood to adolescence. He and his friend Ernie Davis were often teammates until Ernie moved to New York. (They would meet again in 1961 as All-American football players.) When Sandy attended Lafayette JHS, he added playing on the football, basketball, and track teams to his athletic repertoire.

In his youth Sandy could play with the **old** guys because he was a skilled competitor and a valuable member of any team. His contributions and leadership were recognized by everyone in the gymnasium and on the playground. When a pick-up team was being sorted out Sandy was usually one of the "captains" who chose the players. However, actual coaches determined who played on school football teams. Sandy shares below how the actions that friends and a coach took changed the course of his life:

My football career began in 1952 (7th grade) when I finally got a chance to play with most of my friends who were older than me. My early idols were Jim Thorpe, and the great halfbacks, Lenny Moore and Ollie Matson.

There were 18 fellows in the left halfback line and 15 in the right halfback line. A friend who knew how good I could play told me he didn't feel the coaches would have time to assess all my merits at the halfback position and I might not make the team. I was highly insulted and told him I would beat them out anyway! Another friend, who from watching my baseball career, knew I could throw a ball suggested I should try out for quarterback (QB) since there were only two fellows trying out for that position. He thought I could probably beat out the 8th grader and would make the team as a QB and show the coaches my running ability later. I still didn't want any part of my friend's suggestion and was determined to play halfback anyway!

We were all standing in a straight line when the coach called out, "Quarterbacks!" To my surprise and displeasure, the first friend pushed me out front. I was too embarrassed to get back in line, so I decided to give it a try anyway! As my friend predicted, I went on to beat out the 8th grader that year and start as QB in 8th and 9th grades. By the time I reached 10th grade, no one else had enough experience to compete with me.

God has a way of sending us in directions we do not choose, to accomplish great things we cannot envision. Although his reluctance to be embarrassed kept Sandy from returning to his position in the running backs line, he came to realize an athletic path as a quarterback was his destiny. Fellow Uniontown athlete and former running backs' coach for the Indianapolis Colts, Gene Huey, states his appreciation of Sandy's athletic contribution with the following reflection:

There were many great athletes from Uniontown, PA. Sandy was the one through his many accomplishments that put Uniontown on the sports map. He made our town, community, and western PA proud. Never could we be him, but we honor him [by] being like him in our own spirit. (G. Huey––Friend/ Legacy Supporter)

Just as Sandy's friend appreciated his accomplishments, Sandy had considerable admiration for James Francis "Jim" Thorpe (1889-1953), a Sac and Fox Native American athlete from the Oklahoma frontier. Jim Thorpe was awarded gold medals for winning the pentathlon and decathlon events at the 1912 Olympics. He was a multiple sports athlete who was known to build his performance through imitation and visualization. Sandy would use the same methods to sharpen his athletic prowess as he matured.

Jim Thorpe performed feats that remain unparalleled in Olympic history, but he suffered disrespect as a Native American during an era in the United States that was known for discrimination toward people of color. "The International Olympic Committee (IOC) stripped Thorpe of his medals after learning that he had violated the rules of amateurism by playing minor-league baseball in 1909-10. The action was proven prejudicial when it was revealed that white athletes were known to have been similarly paid without any sanction from the IOC." [2] (Jenkins 2012) Sandy was heartbroken by Jim Thorpe's story. He found the action of the IOC unimaginable and patently unfair.

The Jim Thorpe story was compelling and noteworthy but the man and athlete Sandy revered the most from adolescence through manhood was Jackie Robinson (1919-1972). Sandy had joined our parents, grandfather, aunts, and uncles in his love of baseball. They were fans and followers of the Pittsburgh Crawfords and Homestead (PA) Grays of the National Negro League and the extraordinary athletes the league produced, such as Satchel Paige, Josh Gibson, Cool Papa Bell, Judy Johnson, Buck Leonard, and Jackie Robinson.

Jackie Robinson moved from the Kansas City Monarchs to the Brooklyn Dodgers. He was the highly respected baseball player who broke Major League Baseball's color barrier. His opportunity became the defining action that integrated professional baseball and eventually, other professional sports. He was a hero in Black family households. The meaning of his experiences and their impact on society were recognized as culturally significant by our parents. His official biography notes, "Jackie Robinson's life and legacy will be remembered as one of the most important in American history." [3]

Jackie Robinson was an example of how to practice many of the basic tenets we were taught. The way he conducted himself when faced with horrific bigotry, hate, and discrimination served as a model of determination, perseverance, self-assurance, and preparedness for an impressionable young Sandy. He related to the elder Jackie on many levels. Both men were four-sport lettermen––baseball, basketball, football, and track––Sandy in high school and Jackie in college.

Just as Jackie Robinson was the first to break the *color* barrier in American baseball, Sandy dreamed of emulating Jackie by breaking a Division 1 football barrier and becoming an All-American Black quarterback. Furthermore, he saw no reason to limit his dreams to college football recognition. He also aspired to become a franchise Black quarterback in the National Football League (NFL). Sandy believed it was possible to reach the pinnacle of success on both pathways. The dream achieved would result in his life making a difference for future generations and form the foundation of his legacy:

I was in high school when Sandy was making his mark at the University of Minnesota; however, I read with much admiration of his exploits. I was in college in Nebraska during Sandy's glory years and continued following his exploits on TV. I always placed him in the same vein as Jackie Robinson as it related to his pioneering role as a Black quarterback in the Big Ten. His exploits served as inspiration for me to be the best athlete I could be.
(M. Harrison––Friend/Program Director)

Sandy knew his goals would require a lot of work but he was determined to triumph and earn his own trophies––trophies he could display proudly without fear of having them taken away. He resisted responding the way naysayers may have predicted when he was faced with a challenge. Other people's lack of belief in him gave Sandy the incentive to prove them wrong. He was also bolstered by his birth and extended family members who never doubted his ability.

"Family is not defined by biology, or marriage, or even a home. Family are the people you love and who love you back, the people you feel safe around, and the people you can count on to be there when you need them." (_http://cyberparent.com_, Nov.1, 2017) Sandy was known for expressing his love for his family. He believed Ray's athletic capabilities were boundless. He freely admitted that Ray's football pass was so powerful it was hard to catch. Both men excelled in multiple sports throughout their youth in Uniontown and they appreciated hearing cheers of encouragement from the stands.

Sandy considered Joyce and me his most ardent "cheerleaders." We never resisted the cheerleader title because we earned it. We had been shouting from the stands and sidelines for Sandy, Ray, and their Uniontown teammates through victory or defeat since childhood. Much of Sandy's pride was based on our knowledge of the sports we cheered about. Men who joined us to watch a sporting event were pleasantly surprised. Our cheerleading role did not end in Pennsylvania. It continued in Minnesota.

Ray said he heard me yelling his name in Memorial Stadium during a Gopher football spring game. Our love for our brothers and the sports they played will continue until we expire. The Stephens DNA demands it.

Many of the survey comments that referenced Sandy's love for his family are heartwarming:

(Most) Admired personal attributes—His honesty, his belief in himself, his love for his family, and his ability to continue striving for excellence. (C. Attaway (deceased) —Cousin)

He came into my life when I was a teenager. Because I did not grow up with him, the years that we did have together were really treasured. (J. Gloster—Daughter)

Sandy cared about his family. He welcomed me with opened arms and treated me like a son. (T. Gloster—Son-in-law)

Folks should know and remember that the most important thing to Sandy was his family. He loved his brother and sisters and always talked about them and how proud he was of them. (M. Harrison—Friend/Program Director)

(He) Included me in his extended family with no racial overtones. (M. Smith Hudson—MN Friend)

Chapter 2

ADVERSITY

DISCRIMINATION

The treatment of a person or targeted group of people differently,
in a way that is worse than the way people are
usually treated. (dictionary.cambridge.org)

PENNSYLVANIA—PERSONAL CHALLENGES

Sandy's formative years (1940–1954) preceded the modern civil rights era (1954–1968). Being the son of Sanford and Helen Stephens meant he was tutored at a young age in civil rights issues and responsibilities. In addition to their vocations as funeral director and piano/voice teacher, Dad and Mom became known in Uniontown for their civic contributions and educational leadership. They served in the National Association for the Advancement of Colored People (NAACP), Boy Scouts of America, East End Parent Teacher Association (PTA), and many social and fraternal organizations. Dad served as an air raid warden, Mom as a community fund drive coordinator, and both were civil rights activists.

In 1978, at age 38, Sandy penned a letter to the late Carl Rowan, renowned columnist, author, and one of Sandy's mentors. In the letter, Sandy stated, "The greatness of the United States is interwoven into the diverse fabric of its people." It is doubtful that young Sandy found those feelings valued during his first personal bout with discrimination. The incident occurred during a school-sanctioned screening of a movie at one of the town's theaters. Certain epic films such as *Samson and Delilah* (1949) *or Quo Vadis* (1951) were deemed worthy enough to let students leave school to view them.

Sandy and the other then called "colored" students in his school were required to sit in the balcony. The mandate was the device used by theater owners to assure segregation of the "colored" patrons from the "non-colored" patrons seated on the main floor. The theater restriction was not considered a bad thing by the students. The view of the screen was better and there was minimal supervision unless the group became rowdy. One thing that made the separation difficult was not being able to sit with school friends who were "non-colored."

Eventually, the charm of sitting in the balcony was replaced by understanding the meaning and intent of segregation. Our parents and community members taught Sandy, me, and our friends how important it is for Black people to expect and insist on equitable treatment in every instance, but especially when the situation requires paying for services. There was no reason for us to pay full price for a movie ticket, then have limited seating options. The situation changed through community activism. Lesson learned: recognize when we are being discriminated against.

In 1952, his final elementary school year, Sandy had what he describes as his "most devastating early experience with overt discrimination and prejudice." The incident occurred on a trip to Washington, D.C., with the 6th grade schoolboy patrol. Sandy and his Black friends were 9 of the 70 outstanding school patrol members who were rewarded with a trip to the nation's capital by the Uniontown School District. The bus trip up U.S. Route 40 and over the Blue Ridge mountains included passing a historical marker for Negro Mountain. Sandy always maintained that the sign had a less acceptable descriptor that angered him but he put his feelings aside to enjoy the trip. He sat back and interacted with the other boys until they arrived at the upscale hotel where the group would be staying.

Sandy and his friends were told to remain seated when the other patrol members stepped off the bus. At that point, the bile in his throat started rising again. He recognized what was happening and found it unbelievable. He had been looking forward to enjoying the hotel's swimming pool and other amenities. Instead, the nine Black students were transported to a basement apartment in the **Negro** part of town. They received a snack instead of a full course meal when they arrived. After they ate, the nine boys were given a few army coats to double up on to sleep. Sandy was the captain of the East End school patrol. He said, "I was incensed to be personally exposed to the sting of prejudice that was alive and unapologetically acceptable in Washington, D.C."

The next day the group toured the national monuments. Sandy's response to the experience reads:

> As I looked at these hypocritical statements—freedom, justice, and equality, I thought to myself how bad the situation was even here in the nation's capital. And if this was the case here in Washington, D.C., then there was little hope for change in the rest of the country!

A positive outcome of the incident was the reinforcement of one of the principles by which Sandy lived: fight injustice wherever it rears its ugly head. Testimonies include:

> Sandy was a vociferous advocate of equal rights. He never forgot the struggle he went through back in Uniontown, Minnesota and the pros. . . . He was very outspoken about the lack of opportunity given to Black people and athletes. Despite the racial slurs he experienced he always remained very patriotic. (M. Harrison—Friend/Program Director)
>
> [Sandy] believed that if you worked hard, no matter what race or color you are, you would succeed. (G. Bell—Friend/ Brother-in-law)

PENNSYLVANIA—LEADERSHIP

Some level of resistance against racial discrimination, bias, and maltreatment has existed in the USA for centuries. Between 1955 and 1965, when the four of us were in elementary, junior high, and senior high school, a new era in the fight for Black civil rights was in full force. Dad and Mom prepared us for the fight by exposing us to civil rights advocates at rallies in Pittsburgh. Our parents developed strategies to deal with discrimination and bias during the many years they spent living and working in Southern states. They taught us effective non-violent ways to fight against Northern-style bias and discrimination, which tended to be more covert than in the South but just as harmful.

Sandy, our parents, and other community activists in town joined the civil rights fight in Uniontown by participating in sit-ins at five-and-dime-store lunch counters when service was denied. They picketed restaurants that refused admittance or treated certain customers disrespectfully. Movie theater policies were challenged and ultimately changed. Finally, our parents, who had been active YMCA (Y) members and advocates in Pittsburgh, were forced to protest Uniontown YMCA policies that prohibited membership and equal access to services for the Black members of the community. There were no swimming pools in Uniontown and without the Y the nearest swimming opportunity was at the Youghiogheny River Dam located about twenty miles up the mountain on Route 40. We could not take advantage of that swimming opportunity until age 16 when we had our driver's licenses and access to Dad's car.

I was too young to remember the Y discrimination policy, but I took full advantage of access to the pool and other services as soon as I could go downtown unaccompanied. The Y and the library were the only places away from my block that Mom let me visit. For Sandy, the Y was a safer and more sanitary place to swim than the creek that ran through town. My siblings and I all reached swimming proficiency at the Y. Saturdays there became the desired place to gather for swimming, hot dogs, and a movie. By doing so, we encouraged our friends to join us and soon the old policy was replaced with acceptance and inclusion.

One of the many principles we were taught was an obligation to make a difference in the world with our God-given gifts, talents, and intellect. Our parents groomed us to be champions for the improvement of conditions for others. As the eldest, Sandy was expected to lead the way and set an example for the three of us and our friends.

Whether he liked it or not, Sandy was born to be a leader. His friends and family recognized his ability when he was young. As he matured, he did not shy away from the responsibility of leadership. People were not always aware of his natural inclination to be introspective and solitary. The descriptor I prefer to use for both of us is extroverted introvert. Sandy was very comfortable spending solitary time with a musical background. He was also very gregarious. When people offered him a choice of being led or taking the lead, Sandy chose leadership without hesitation. Several friends and colleagues provided the following examples of Sandy's aptitude to lead in response to the survey question, "What personal attributes did Sandy exhibit that you admired?"

> We were all pioneers back then. Our moms and dads set the standards for all of us. But Sandy was a true leader back home because he set a positive example for our whole community. He showed the bigots that Blacks could not only be great athletes but were very intelligent to boot. (M. Cohen—Friend/Legacy Supporter)
>
> Competitive, great athlete. Stayed centered. Didn't let his being well known go to his head. (B. Dillard—Long-time Friend/ Coach)
>
> Confidence! He was a true leader. [I am an] Air Force General, and [I know] he was the type of person we ask for as a leader. (D. Schulstad—Fan)
>
> Sandy was not afraid to take a leadership role on the football team, which was made up of mostly white athletes. (J. Robinson—Friend/Alpha Brother)

Once he faced his fate as a leader of others, Sandy devoted himself to dispelling the myth that he was not capable of the leadership role. He assumed the responsibility and found ways to help others believe in his vision for success.

MINNESOTA —AWARENESS

Sandy intended to express his feelings about Minnesota and racial discrimination in his autobiography. His words reveal his passion about both:

> The **Sandy Stephens** story has been the subject of many magazine articles. The story was featured on *Tony Brown's Journal* in the winter of 1979, as the program, "Gold Is Also

Black." My experience is a microcosm within a macrocosm of unjustified discrimination that has existed in the United States for decades. Exposing the fallacy of racial discrimination and bias has been my lifelong goal.

The following events took place in 1994: 1) In Eden Prairie last spring a cross was burned on the lawn of an Afro-American family! The community rose up and declared they weren't going to tolerate this behavior from its residents! 2) Recently, an Afro-American was shot in a Blaine mall while just walking through the mall! 3) A rally was held in St. Paul declaring "Prejudice Isn't Welcome," (WCCO) Ch.4, Monday, Oct. 10, 1994! 4) The same day a teenager was shot and killed at Harding High School. 5) Also, the same day, there were racial riots in London, England! 6) Oct. 1, 1994, after the Gophers vs. Indiana game in Bloomington, Indiana, the news reported a KKK rally at the courthouse in Lafayette, Indiana! I had a ray of hope when the police had to escort the clan out of town because white residents were outraged by this behavior!

At the same time, Dennis Green is the Head Coach and Warren Moon is the quarterback of the Minnesota Vikings; Dr. McKinley Boston is the Athletic Director for the Univ. of Minnesota; and S.E.E.D. (Seeking Educational Equity and Diversity) training for teachers is taking place throughout the school systems.

I never regretted coming to Minnesota because I felt it had the best standard of living of any state in the USA. I eventually moved my entire family here. I have a love affair with the State, the fans, and the Metro Area! There is still much room for improvement in the Twin Cities Metro Area and the entire state, but we are still at the forefront in providing equal opportunity to all its citizens, regardless of their race, creed, color, or religion. I am very proud of the achievements and stature I have attained in this great state. I want to give something back to Minnesota because the state has been so good to me.

When I took up the task of writing the book, I realized there was so much more I wanted to say pertaining to the times and ordeals of my people, and how I wanted to bring to light many aspects of social inequality, not just my football escapades.
Sandy Stephens

INJUSTICE

The unjust or prejudicial treatment of different categories of people or things, especially on the grounds of race, age, or sex. (https://www.en.oxforddictionaries.com)

PENNSYLVANIA—PAIN

Sandy's youthful encounter with injustice and prejudice was undeniable and personal. When he was a teenager, Sandy's athletic life revolved around baseball. He was a switch hitter who could hit the ball 400 feet either right-handed or left-handed. Sandy's contribution to the talented Veterans of Foreign Wars (VFW) baseball team gave him the opportunity to travel to Hershey, Pennsylvania to compete in the Pennsylvania (PA) baseball championship for players 13 to 15 years of age.

An Olympic-size swimming pool was visible from the hotel room where the team was staying. Sandy, a YMCA shark-level swimmer by that age, was looking forward to executing his trademark swan dive into the water to win the admiration of the other players and any female onlookers. When Sandy stepped up to pay for admission to the pool, he was refused. The person in the booth did not give a reason for the refusal, he simply would not accept Sandy's money and effectively barred his entry. One of Sandy's teammates asked to speak to the manager. The manager said the other players were allowed in the pool, but Sandy was not because he was "colored." In protest, everyone on the team refused to swim, demanded their money back, and did not go to the pool for the remainder of the trip.

Sandy felt the guys on the already great team jelled into a bonded unit after the incident. The players reflected the brotherhood that develops among teammates. They showed everyone their strength as a team by capturing the PA State Baseball Championship. To a man, the team reinforced the message Sandy had been taught about the caliber of human beings. Dad and Mom emphasized that a person should be measured by their deeds, rather than their words. Sandy appreciated having his worth measured by his capabilities and integrity. He was surrounded by men of character whose actions counteracted the ignorance of others.

The ugly head of injustice (and prejudice) did not intrude into Sandy's sports career again until his senior year in high school. He had decided to accept invitations to two of the three all-star games his football stardom had earned. The first event was the East-West Penn All-Star Game. Sandy was the starting quarterback for the East squad. He was looking forward to competing with and against athletes who were highly accomplished. He was excused from the training camp to attend an awards ceremony in Fayette County.

The Fayette County Annual Awards ceremony was held to recognize the best all-around athletes from high schools in the county, including Uniontown JSHS. Sandy's record in multiple sports made him eligible to receive more than one award, including the prestigious Outstanding Athlete of Fayette County. He expected the challenge for the awards to come from his Uniontown teammates or competitors in his division. Uniontown had a triple A (AAA) conference rating because of its size and level of competition. He did not expect the players from double A (AA) or single A rated schools to pose a problem because in his opinion, comparing their competition levels to Uniontown's schedule would be equivalent to comparing the Ohio Valley Conference with the Big Ten Conference. Sandy and Dad were looking forward to a rewarding evening.

During the ceremony, Sandy was named Uniontown's outstanding athlete and he was, "gratified and humbled" by the recognition. His accomplishments included: **Football**: Quarterback, 1st team All-State and Wigwam All-American; **Basketball**: 3rd team All-State and section scoring leader; **Track**: most individual points in the county track meet; and **Baseball**: tryouts with the Pittsburgh Pirates and Philadelphia Phillies. Sandy believed no one deserved to receive Fayette County's biggest trophy more than he did.

Other awards were presented and Sandy was nervous with anticipation. Finally, the time came for the big announcement. The emcee stepped to the microphone and shouted, "The winner of the Outstanding Athlete of Fayette County is _____." It was not Sandy's name! His heart sank, his eyes watered, and he steeled himself to stay upright. For the first time in his athletic career, he felt the sting of injustice and he was helpless to do anything except accept it. He could not pin the loss directly on prejudice, but the decision inflicted a weight of sadness on him that he had never experienced before. Dad was upset for his son and expressed his anger with colorful expletives, but both men held their heads high and moved forward to congratulate the winner.

The perceived Fayette County slight resulted in another turning point for Sandy. It was the first time he wondered what level of talent he would need to exhibit to gain respect as a Black athlete. He knew inequitable treatment and injustices would occur but his responses to them needed to reflect the principles and teachings of his childhood and inform his adult decisions. He determined that his best course of action was to keep doing what he had been doing, show up and show out athletically. Performing at his best was the way to keep ascending toward his personal promised land.

After the crushing disappointment of not being named the Fayette County athlete of the year, Sandy turned his attention to quarterback duties for the East-West Penn All-Star game and the Big 33 All-Star Game. The inaugural Big 33 All-Star Game pitted 33 Pennsylvania high school All-State athletes against a team of high school All-Americans from the 47 other states in the United States. Bernie Bierman, Hall of Fame coach from the University of Minnesota, was the coach for the Pennsylvania All-Stars.

The site of the Big 33 game was Hershey, PA. The town held painful memories for Sandy from his experience there in 1953 as a baseball player. However, during the years since his swimming pool incident, integration laws had gone into effect. The advancement in social consciousness resulted in all participants of the Big 33 All-Star Game enjoying the amenities of the lodge where they stayed. Sandy made it a point to dive and swim laps in the formerly forbidden swimming pool.

Sandy's teammates included his friend and future roommate Judge Dickson. Judge and the other members of the team provided a morale boost and affirmation for Sandy when they chose him to be one of the team captains. They believed his leadership style and capabilities would lead them to victory. The team's faith in Sandy was not misplaced. He was instrumental in leading the Pennsylvania All-Stars to a victory in the 1957 Big 33 All-Star Game. He felt vindicated and never traveled to Hershey, PA, again.

PERCEPTION

A way of regarding, understanding, or interpreting
something; a mental impression. *(Dictionary.com)*

An important contribution to the discussion of the perception of Black
men in society is Marlene Kim Conner's book *What Is Cool?*[1] (Connor
2003) We were working with Marlene prior to Sandy's demise in 2000. She
shared a draft of her then pending book for his review. Sandy took copious
notes as he read. They include these excerpts from the book's epilogue:

Race is a smokescreen and a handy way to manipulate whole
groups of people, to get them to focus elsewhere, anywhere
other than where the real problems lie.

Black man——it's not about getting paid——that doesn't make
you a man. It's a country determined **not** to pay you and to
define what a man is in such a way as to deprive you of that
title.

"Cool" is about becoming a man! Becoming a man is
about succeeding by the dictates of your environment. It is
determined by your peer group, your family, your point of view
and perspective. A Black boy's way of becoming a man is in his
environment with the requisite and well-deserved self-esteem
and respect that comes with manhood!

ROLE MODELS

Sandy was aware of the perception in the 1950s that Black men
should feel privileged to be a member of a team and to follow the lead of
others more capable of decision making. This perception was based on
societal norms in the USA. It permeated more than sports and perpetuated
the white supremacy myth for centuries. Football was symbolic of the
perception. The men in positions of power in amateur and professional
football were not reticent about admitting that Black men could run fast
enough, catch well enough, jump high enough, and were durable enough

to be on the team, but they maintained that Black men were not intelligent enough to lead a team or be accepted in a leadership role by predominantly white teammates.

> . . . possibly as impactful as that false perception was the amount of attention and fanfare afforded the quarterback. Such attention holds true for all leaders, whatever the competition—— war or sport. **Sandy Stephens**

In other words, a talented Black man who exuded confidence in his skills and accomplishments and was not shy about assuming a proud attitude about his skills should have been willing to keep a low profile— stay in his place and resist attracting too much attention. Sandy was never willing to fit into a mold crafted by others who doubted his worth. In Western PA the most capable athlete for a position was given the opportunity to play. The quarterback position was no exception. Sandy kept getting confirmation that exhibiting the best skill set was the key to acceptance. He was an 18-year-old Black man with a plan. He also was too honest to act as if he was not one of the best competitors in any contest.

Although Sandy recognized his capabilities, he lacked enough information about successful Black quarterbacks to use as role models. He might have gained more insights if he had been guided to research the following men:

> ➤ **Fritz Pollard (1894–1986),** HOF '05, the first Black man to play in the Rose Bowl, first to play in the backfield (quarterback) in the pre-WW II era in the NFL, and first head coach in the NFL with the Akron Pros in 1921.[2] (The editors of Encyclopedia Britannica 2004)
>
> ➤ Excerpt from Kwame McDonald article "Pollard finally inducted into NFL Hall of Fame."[3] (McDonald 2005)

Dr. Frederick Douglas "Fritz" Pollard of Brown University and the Akron Pros, after being passed over 42 times by the National Football League Hall of Fame selectors, was finally enshrined in the hall on Saturday, August 7, 2005. Even as the former Brown University alum is enshrined, the coverage of the 2005 class of Hall of Fame inductees looks as though only two quarterbacks were deserving of the coveted induction. According to our local media outlets, Dan Marino and Steve Young were the only deserving players to be installed this year. . . .In addition to his tardy induction into the hall, Pollard was mistreated by fans and game opponents alike. He often had to dress in his car and be ushered into the stadium by security guards. . . .

➢ **George Taliaferro (1927–2018),** HOF '81, the first Black man drafted by the NFL, LA Dons in 1949. In seven NFL seasons, Taliaferro played an unheard-of seven positions: quarterback, running back, wide receiver, punter, kick returner, punt returner, and defensive back.[4] (Bembry 2017)

Excerpt from *George Taliaferro played quarterback and a whole lot more.*[5] *(Bembry 2017)*

As a freshman at Indiana University in Bloomington, IN, Taliaferro wasn't happy. "I felt like a fifth-class citizen. Being educated is not only the acquisition of knowledge," he said, "but the understanding of what's going on in the world and learning to conduct yourself with and among people of all races." When Taliaferro asked the football coaches when he was going to be moved on campus, he was told black students didn't live in dorms.

"I called my father and told him I didn't want to be in a place where I couldn't live on campus, where I couldn't swim in the pool, and where I couldn't sit in the bottom section of the movie theater," Taliaferro said. "My father told me there were other reasons I was there, and then he hung up the phone on me. I was never so hurt because I thought the one person who could understand being discriminated against was him."

The period between Sandy's and George Taliaferro's experiences spanned 30 years, yet their experiences had noticeable similarities regarding the ways they were treated by others and their responses to that treatment.

> **Willie Thrower (1930–2002),** HOF '05, the first Black man to play quarterback at a Big Ten conference school in the post-WW II era. He accepted a one-year contract with the Chicago Bears and broke a major racial barrier in the National Football League when on October 18, 1953, he was called in as a substitute quarterback in a game against the San Francisco 49ers.[6] (Reid 2017)

I do not know how much knowledge Sandy had of these men but I believe he would have appreciated how much their perseverance and endurance in athletics and their influence on the world around them represented models of behavior for him to emulate.

Sandy did not believe a coach could discern that the quarterback they were scouting was a fair-skinned Black man who had outstanding football knowledge and skill. I think he underestimated how much information coaches shared about the backgrounds of potential athletes, including ethnicity. Nevertheless, ability needed to be the primary factor scouts and coaches considered if they intended to give each potential student athlete an opportunity to attend their school and become a star performer.

Family and friends were aware of the historical impact Sandy's selection to play the quarterback position in the Big Ten Conference would have on the sport and the country. A sampling of their perspectives is shared here:

I remember receiving a telephone call from Sandy's mom (the late Helen Stephens) telling me that the family was in Columbus, Ohio, and that Sandy would be interviewed by the ("late, great") Woody Hayes, coach for the Ohio State University football team. We were all filled with pride because we realized that Sandy was being offered an opportunity few African Americans had been given during that time period. (C. Attaway (deceased)––Cousin)

His determination to prove that he possessed the intelligence and ability to change the perception that a black man could not master the quarterback position at the highest level. (M. Hickenbottom––Lifelong friend)

He was a first and a (next level) Black athlete in Minnesota. He raised the bar for this position in 1960 and 1961 and it has not been equaled since. Warmath was about 5 years ahead of Bryant (Alabama) in recruiting blacks for D1 football. (B. Mchie ––Fan/Historian)

Sandy left big footsteps to be filled even at the high school level. Playing quarterback at Maryland State I wanted to make the team, so I would imitate Sandy by doing his classic bootleg. I would do this to impress the coaches. He was the standard. (C. Thomas––Extended Family)

Future Gophers Sandy and fellow Pennsylvanian Judge Dickson signed their national letters of intent in our living room in Uniontown. It was very exciting. The rest of the family knew where Minnesota was on the map but other than extremely cold winters, we did not have much information about the demographics or culture of the state. We had no idea at that time how immersed in the culture we would become.

Sandy became aware of how progressive Big Ten recruitment policies were regarding Black quarterbacks. He shared his discovery with Mom in a letter during his freshman year:

Hi Mom,

. . .

I've discovered that I won't be the first Black QB in the Big Ten, because the second school I received an offer from, Wisconsin, has one. His name is Sidney Williams and he is truly outstanding. We rode the train down to Madison and saw him start as the QB for three quarters, then they switched him to halfback. The same old story!

Much more to my surprise is noting that two other schools are starting QB's as sophomores. The University of Illinois has Mel Meyers, a gifted athlete who can pass well and with 9.7 seconds sprinting speed, he is a running threat. The University of Iowa plays Wilburn Hollis, a highly touted athlete out of Boys' Town in Nebraska. Wilburn is a dynamic QB who can pass, run, and scramble well, but most important, he is always poised in adverse situations and will invariably come up with the big play.

I often ponder what future encounters we might have opposing each other on the field as generals. Your loving son, Sandy

---

The men referenced throughout this section operated under the football one-platoon system. The system was used when the game originated because teams only had a few players and each man had to play on both sides of the ball——offense and defense. Sandy was a skilled runner, passer, kick returner, and punter. The athletes Sandy admired and researched were Otto Graham of Cleveland Browns fame and Notre Dame stars King Hill and Paul Hornung. They were best known as quarterbacks and running backs, but they also served as place kicker, punter, kick returner, etc. Sandy studied how they performed at their various positions intending to imitate them, then improve on their moves with his unique skill set.

At the University of Minnesota, punting skills played a part in Sandy's success. The trainer told him that based on the laws of physiology he should not be able to lift his leg as high as he did. Obviously, his physiological gifts and work ethic, on and off the field, paid dividends for Sandy.

Coach Warmath shared, "Sandy was just as good defensively as he was offensively. He was good enough to be our quarterback, do our throwing, do our punting, kickoffs, and kick for extra points. He did everything. He was a great, great, great football player; one of the finest I have ever coached."[7]

Sandy's determination is one reason why there are so many Black quarterbacks. (T. Gloster——Son-in-law)

I admired Sandy for his determination to play quarterback at a major college. I took the easy road and decided to play at an all-Black college in Alabama, where I felt there would be less racial tension. (J. Robinson——Friend/Alpha Brother)

Chapter 3

ROSE BOWL DREAM

DETERMINATION

Firm or fixed intention to achieve a desired end.
(https://www.merriam-webster.com)

In 1958 Sandy and Judge moved into the newly built Territorial Hall on the Minneapolis campus. The roommates made several solemn oaths. They recommitted to the resolution they made in Uniontown to never second-guess their decision to enroll in the University of Minnesota. They also intended to lead the Gophers to a level of success the team had not achieved in decades. Both young men had used their fierce, competitive spirits to reach the goals they had set for themselves to date. The university experience would help them fulfill their dreams at the next level.

Story of a Rose Bowl Dream!!
(Sandy Stephens)

1. Teammates laughed when I put a picture of the Rose Bowl up over my desk. They thought I was crazy to even dream about it.
2. Existing players didn't believe we could get to the Rose Bowl because in the history of the school they hadn't achieved this goal.
3. I knew why they had lost in prior years! They didn't believe they could win!

Sandy and Judge pointed to the picture of the Rose Bowl on the wall and asked team members who visited their room if they believed playing in the Rose Bowl was possible. Sandy's sense of brotherhood, teamwork, and camaraderie was an important element of his belief system and personality. It took some time but eventually the other team members embraced his Rose Bowl vision and determined to work hard to reach their common goal. Competitive fire and determination were basic qualities Sandy possessed that family, friends, and fans recognized:

> The quiet and strong persona always embodied the burning passion to compete and win, no matter how insurmountable the odds may have seemed to be. (G. Huey––Friend/Legacy Supporter)

> I didn't know him well, but I loved his competitive fire and style. (D. Butwin––Former MN DAILY Sports Editor/ Reporter)

At the dinner for freshman players to get acquainted, most of the attention in the room was focused on Sandy and Judge since they were the newest, highly recruited out-of-towners. The two friends joined Bob McNeil as the three Black athletes on the team. Bob was thrilled to no longer be alone. Each new player gave his name and position. When Sandy proclaimed his position as a quarterback, the murmuring and buzzing voices he expected happened. Sandy was not sidetracked by their skepticism. Nothing could dim his belief in his vision of playing in the Rose Bowl. He knew he was blazing new trails. A family adage from our youth was, "talk is cheap; what you do is what counts." No minds would be changed if he did not back up his declaration with exceptional performance on the field.

PRIDE

The quality or state of being proud; a reasonable or justifiable
self-respect; marked by stateliness, magnificence.
(https://www.merriam-webster.com)

Sandy always took pride in his athletic ability. He was also very
fastidious and conscious of the impression he made on others with his
persona and appearance. One of the interesting stories about Sandy's first
days as a Minnesota Gopher football player may seem trivial, but the
situation and Sandy's response to it are symbolic of how strongly he felt
about making a positive impression, looking dapper, and problem-solving.
His vision of what was presentable for football team picture day was met
with a potentially career-ending challenge.

The incident involved Coach Warmath's never-to-be-challenged
decree that players were not allowed to wear low-cut shoes. Sandy tells us
what happened:

Finally, the day of the first practice arrived. Naturally, I was
one of the first to the locker room to get all my equipment
just right. This day was also to be picture day, which meant I
wanted to be extra sharp when I entered the field. Then came
my first disappointment. It made me think I had made the
wrong choice and my coach and I were not going to get along
too well, which would in turn hurt my chances of playing. As
we went to get our issue of shoes, the equipment manager said,
"The coach doesn't allow anybody to wear low-cut shoes." I
couldn't understand what in the world he was talking about. I
had never worn anything but low cuts since 7th grade! It would
just seem degrading and backward to wear big cumbersome
high-tops––for any reason.

The uniforms were dingy and lackluster as it was, I thought.
To wear high-tops too, and on picture day especially, was too
much to bear! Like the Gillette razor blade advertisement at
the time, I believed a player had to "look sharp, to feel sharp,
to play sharp." In order to circumvent this order, I went back
in the locker room and put on the shoes I had brought from

high school. Many of the other players were upset also, but most were afraid to wear their own shoes because of the order.

I wasn't doing it to appear different or anything, but I knew I couldn't perform as well in those big ol' high-tops and I definitely didn't want my picture taken in them. So, I went out to the practice field and began to warm up. Coach Warmath called me over and asked me why I had low cuts on after his order. I explained how I felt to him, but to no avail. He explained that on the previous picture day, the starting quarterback and another starter had sprained their ankles therefore the order was going to hold fast. I remember going back to the locker room to change and I was so mad I wanted to cry, fight, and quit. After sitting down and thinking about the options I had, I realized there were none. I couldn't quit under any circumstances, yet to have my first picture taken looking like a lineman was just unbearable to think of.

Finally, after being in the locker room too long I knew I had to do something. Then it hit me. The camera might not get a good shot at the shoes if I was moving in an action shot. So, I got some white shoestrings to replace the dingy black shoestrings that were in the shoes and I rolled the high-tops down to low cut length. If I got sent back again, my last move was to tape over the high-tops à la Lenny Moore style. Once again, I entered the field and by now all the players and coaches were watching to see how I would look upon my return. My jaws were quite rigid and at this point I didn't want to hear anything from anybody.

I trotted slowly back onto the field and suddenly, before the coach could say anything, Judge burst out laughing. He knew my pride was shattered and there I was in high-tops, but I had rolled them down. Everyone, including the coaches, began laughing although I didn't see a damn thing funny at the time. Then my nickname for the next week was "High-tops." I bitterly disliked the name and was worried that it might stick with me throughout my college career.

Ultimately, as the week progressed, I got my wish to wear low cut shoes. I explained that I couldn't punt with high-tops on. Coach Warmath knew my displeasure, but he couldn't back down now since so much fuss had been made over the issue. So, in order to make us both happy, he made the punters exceptions to the high-top shoe ruling. The change only exempted three players, and I was one of them.

SANFORD E. STEPHENS
FUNERAL HOME

TEAMWORK

Work done by several associates with each doing a part but all subordinating personal prominence to the efficiency of the whole. (https://www.merriam-webster.com)

This book's introduction shares the story of the impressive performance of the players in Memorial Stadium that led to Sandy's nickname. One element of the 1959 scrimmage was the unexpected successful pairing of Sandy and George Meissner (a.k.a. Mize), a reserve teammate. When George tells the story with passion and precision, a person with football knowledge can visualize the action. It was the most memorable day in his U of MN athletic experience. Mize and Sandy teamed up to complete a 32-yard touchdown and the two-point conversion that followed. They continued their stellar performance when Mize put a textbook block on the defensive end and opened a gap in the line for Sandy to burst through and cross the goal line for a 35-yard touchdown. It was great fun and the team cheered them on as they congratulated each other.

Congratulations was not on Coach Warmath's lips. He ran a "tight ship" and since he had not called either play Sandy and George had executed, Coach was upset. Both players were reprimanded and they were not given another opportunity to play together. Nevertheless, Mize never forgot the opportunity Sandy showed to an **undervalued** teammate. Years later, George penned the lyrics and music to his tribute song:

UNIONTOWN

Sept. 19, 1959 – True Story
By George Allan Meissner, "Mize"
8/23/2007

His name is Sandy Stephens, from Uniontown, PA.
He was something Special, I do have to say;
He was Big and Powerful, and he could throw the ball;
His name is Sandy Stephens, NUMBER 15's ON THE WALL.

He came to Minnesota in the fall of '58.
He carried his umbrella in a very Special way;
Sandy, he was charming, HE ALWAYS DREW A CROWD;
He took care of business; he would go that extra mile.

September 19. '59, on the final scrimmage day,
A starting end got injured, so Mize went in the game;
Sandy called his number, on the first play;
A 32-yard touchdown, what else can they say?

And much to Mize' surprise, Sandy came right back to he.
A 2-point conversion, Yes, Sandy nailed thee.
The Kicker, he was injured, or he would have kicked for one;
So, Sandy gave the Mize, His Big Day in The Sun.

George is adamant about preserving Sandy's place in sports history. He remains a supporter whose friendship reflects Sandy's belief in the worth of a teammate.

DEVELOPMENT

To lead or conduct (something) through a succession of states or changes each of which is preparatory for the next.
(https://www.merriam-webster.com)

The Gophers' resolve to play in the "Big Daddy" of all the bowl games was tested during the 1959 season. The glory the sophomore-laden team had experienced during the final scrimmage did not last. Sandy characterized the season as the "sophomore-year blues." The team's losing record of 2 wins and 7 losses put the Gophers in last place in the Big Ten Conference. The record was excruciatingly painful for Sandy. He had not experienced many losses in his high school athletic experience and he hated it. Making matters worse, six of the seven losses were by a margin of 6 points or less. In Sandy's mind the margin reflected an inexperienced team that made too many mistakes.

The media coverage of the unfortunate team record was direct and painful. The recruitment of the Black players was deemed a mistake in terms that showed unfiltered prejudice and bias. The columnists did not know that Sandy was hurt to the point of crying after the Illinois game. He and his teammates knew they were better than their record reflected. They needed to keep working and attracting more outstanding players to become a winning team.

Sandy and Judge were instrumental in recruiting additional talented athletes. Two freshman players, Bill Munsey, Sandy's friend from Uniontown, and Bobby Bell from North Carolina were among them. The four men and their teammates were destined to make history together.

The young men were riding through campus when they saw an effigy of Coach Warmath hanging under the Washington Avenue footbridge. Sandy and Judge felt the effigy was directed at them. Once more they made a vow to show Minnesota fans and reporters how wrong they were to question Coach Warmath's decision to recruit football players from elite athlete hotbeds such as Western Pennsylvania, North Carolina, Ohio, Virginia, and other states.

News sources reported that Coach Warmath was being attacked at every level but Coach's players were not exposed to his personal pain. He expected them to continue their workouts, practices, and studies as if nothing else was happening. Sandy praised his coach for being a prime example of an *If* man:

Living through this incredible experience made me appreciate and respect this man and coach, Murray Warmath, as a man and teacher of life and how to respond to it. Against many adversities he never wavered and went about business as usual. Garbage was dumped on his lawn, his children had to be taken out of school, and his wife couldn't shop at the supermarket. These many years later, Coach Warmath has never complained or even mentioned these horrible, atrocious occurrences. What a role model!

MOVING FORWARD

The 1960 Gopher Football season was triumphant. The team honors included the Big Ten Co-Championship, the National Football Championship, and the coveted invitation to the Rose Bowl. The previously critical press and skeptical fans were proven wrong in their rush to judgment of Coach Warmath and his young team. A year of hard work and maturation revealed their true talent. Sandy received Consensus All-America honor and was fourth in the Heisman Trophy voting. He was thrilled to be the first Black quarterback to attain All-American status. His joy was compounded ten-fold when his boyhood friend, Ernie Davis, became the first Black athlete to win the Heisman Trophy. The men represented their hometown with honor and distinction.

Many articles have been written about the only Gopher teams to earn invitations to the Rose Bowl. Instead of repeating those perspectives, the family back-stories will be shared in these pages.

PENNSYLVANIA--ROSE BOWL #1

Uniontown family, friends, and fans cheered as loudly as the Minnesota Golden Gopher community when Sandy and the football team were invited to the Rose Bowl to compete against the Washington Huskies. We all were aware of Sandy's dream of playing there. Mom and Dad started making plans to go to Pasadena for the game. Our home was buzzing with anticipation. Christmas was celebrated, but the festivities took a back seat to what was going to happen New Year's Day.

Dad, Mom, and Bill Munsey's parents, Mr. George and "Miz" Evelyn, flew to California to join in the excitement. Once again, I was relegated to the role of funeral home attendant which left me unhappy. Dad and Mom called from the intersection of Hollywood and Vine in Los Angeles, California, at midnight. They were bringing in 1961 with Gopher fans and thousands of other revelers. Ray and Joyce were at a party and I was staring at the Christmas tree, alone. Not a fun time. I expected my mood to change dramatically on New Year's Day when the Gophers were crowned the Rose Bowl champions.

Unfortunately, the Gophers lost to Washington 17-7 and Sandy had a dismal game that included 3 interceptions. Those results were not how he envisioned his performance in the Rose Bowl after waiting so many years to make the trip. We were devastated. The one bright spot was seeing Bill Munsey score the only Gopher touchdown. I was doubly upset that I could not be at the game to console Sandy, not with words, but with my presence. His quest to debunk the myth about Black quarterback skills by showing exceptional leadership and conquering the Rose Bowl pinnacle of success was shattered. Sandy was known for his resilience, but this defeat would leave a scar. I was very happy Mom and Dad were there to comfort him.

A pamphlet written by Charles Loftus titled, *What Is a Football Player?* is poetic and compelling. The writer's description of a football player is in sync with the feelings Sandy expressed in his writings, presentations, and interviews. The following excerpt can help a non-player understand how the players may have felt after the 1961 Rose Bowl loss:

> *A football player is a wonderful creature – you can criticize him, but you can't discourage him. You can defeat his team, but you can't make him quit. You can get him out of a game, but you can't get him out of football. Might as well admit it – be you an alumnus, coach or fan – he is your personal representative on the field, your symbol of fair and hard play. He may not be an All-American, but he is an example of the American way. He is judged not for his race, not for his religion, not for his social standing, or not for his finances, but by the democratic yardstick of how well he blocks, tackles, and sacrifices individual glory for the overall success of the team.*
>
> *He is a hard-working untiring, determined kid doing the best he can for his school or college. And when you come out of a stadium grousing and feeling upset that your team lost, he can make you mighty ashamed with two sincerely spoken words – "we tried!"[1] (Loftus 1951)*

Sandy and the Gopher team rebounded from the Rose Bowl loss by continuing their winning ways in the 1961 season. Sandy and Judge had helped to infuse a passion to win in their teammates when they were freshmen. They set the goal of going to the Rose Bowl and they accomplished the goal but came up short of the victory. Now they were experiencing another stellar season and they felt worthy of the accolades they received. Their success helped to put any remaining disbelievers in their place. Among the honors members of the team received was a plaque Sandy cherished. It reads, "1961 Oregon Club Award to Sandy Stephens, Football, University of Minnesota. Awarded annually to the Outstanding Athlete to compete against a University of Oregon team." Sandy loved being recognized for his competitive prowess. Competing to be the best was a basic part of his system.

TRIUMPH

The act, fact, or condition of being victorious or triumphant;
a significant success or noteworthy achievement.
(dictionary.com)

The Minnesota Gopher football team played for pride during the 1961 season. They did not expect to get another chance to play for Rose Bowl glory regardless of their winning record. There was a mandate at the time that prohibited Big Ten teams from getting back-to-back invitations. The team's excellent fitness and preparation served the Gophers well when the U of MN received an invitation to play in the 1962 Rose Bowl in place of the Ohio State Buckeyes––the Big Ten champions. The Ohio State administration had declined the invitation.

PENNSYLVANIA––ROSE BOWL #2 VIEWING PARTY

The day of the game found the Stephens homestead buzzing again. The game was televised and we had a Rose Bowl party. Family and friends covered all the furniture and the floor in the living room. It was standing room only. The game was exciting. No one in the room was surprised by how well Sandy played. God had given him another chance to fulfill his dream and no mere squad of opponents would be able to defeat him and the imposing group of men with him. Not this time!

Mom was sitting in her rocking chair in the doorway of the living room. At a point in the excitement when we had not heard her voice for a few minutes, we looked at the spot where she should have been and realized Mom had rocked the chair backward to the edge of the stairs.

One more rock would send her toppling backward down the steps. We stopped everything long enough to make her aware of her situation and get her back to safety.

Sandy was a force to be reckoned with on every level. UCLA prepared to counteract his reputation as an option quarterback but they underestimated his capacity to call plays that would disrupt their defensive plan. He also added headaches to the opponent's defense by using his run option and completing two personal touchdown plays. Sandy used all the weapons in his arsenal of football knowledge to lead his team to success. He was named the MVP (Most Valuable Player) of the game and joined Coach Warmath as the Minnesota representatives on the Rose Bowl "wall of fame."

Chapter 4

CONNECTIONS

FRATERNITY

A group of people associated or formally organized for a
common purpose, interest, or pleasure.
(https://www.merriam-webster.com)

As Sandy and the other football recruits struggled to build their
reputations in the football community, campus fraternities were busy
trying to entice the men to join their ranks. In 1961 Bob McNeil prompted
his teammates Sandy Stephens, Bill Munsey, Bobby Bell, and Carl Eller to
join him as pledges in Alpha Phi Alpha (A Φ A) fraternity. Sandy's decision
to pledge reflected his attitudes and frames of reference. He believed in the
Alpha Phi Alpha (Alpha) goals of service to others in the community and
the desire to help Black students at the U of MN succeed academically and
thrive in the university environment. Fraternity life can be the epitome of
brotherhood on a university campus. For these men it represented a group
of Black men with whom they could bond. An article in the fraternity's
May 1961 issue of the *Sphinx Magazine* expressed the fraternity's pride
about their new pledges:

MORE POWER TO THIS PLEDGE CLUB

"After comparative inactivity since 1956 due to the small
enrollment of persons aspiring to become members of Alpha Phi
Alpha in the Twin Cities, a pledge club has been formed at the
University of Minnesota, which shows promise. The pledges,
whose good deeds and activities are rapidly becoming common

topics of conversation, are sparking social and civic activities on the U of M campus as well as in St. Paul and Minneapolis.

These men are, almost to a man, of unusually high caliber and boundless energy, presenting a constant challenge for their pledge master. They, aptly guided by the Twin Cities graduate chapter Gamma Xi Lambda, have given several successful parties; completed a club project of raising five hundred dollars through a benefit dance for a young boy who has since had a successful open-heart operation; and they aspire to become good Alpha men and to be members of the first Negro fraternity to have a frat house on the campus of the University of Minnesota.

On many campuses a house is a commonplace thing, but Minnesota is far removed from the big civic centers where Alpha life flourishes; however, things are changing, and this is the largest pledge club to-date and their goal is now a possibility.
. . .
This pledge club consists of four varsity players of our great Minnesota team that went to the Rose Bowl last fall as well as five hopefuls for the 1961 team. We also have pledged several academic giants and three track men, including one who does the sixty-yard dash in six seconds. This pledge club has been in existence only three months and their dedication to purpose is best expressed by their joint desire to become well enough equipped to be the nucleus of an effort to stimulate in Negro students at the University of Minnesota a desire for participation in greater scholastic achievement, civic responsibility and the creation of a means to a joyful social life often not found at Big Ten schools but inseparable from a happy college experience."

CAMPUS CHALLENGES

Furthering the Alpha Phi Alpha goals and aspirations was difficult in the climate at the U of MN in 1961. The U of MN administration did not permit fraternities and sororities of color to own or reside as a group in off-campus houses. The groups were likewise restricted to gathering in certain areas on campus such as the second floor of Coffman Union. All other campus spots were prohibited. A positive outcome of the restrictions was the opportunity for the young people to build friendships and network with influential Black community leaders and citizens in St. Paul and Minneapolis. Sandy and his Alpha brothers met notable people including Carl Rowan, Pulitzer Prize journalist; Roy Wilkins, civil rights activist; L. Howard Bennett, judge (a former Fisk classmate of Mom); Hobart T. Mitchell, realtor; Cecil B. Newman, newspaper publisher, and many others. Fraternity and sorority brothers and sisters accepted the hospitality offered by social clubs, recreation centers, and community centers, such as Hallie Q. Brown in St. Paul and Phyllis Wheatley House in Minneapolis. They found safe, welcoming venues to hold meetings, sponsor events, and provide service to the Black community. Sandy remained an active Alpha man throughout his life.

One of Sandy's Alpha brothers shares:

> He had a great sense of humor and was a great fraternity brother during his earlier years. (J. Robinson––Friend/Alpha Brother)

BARBARA R. STEPHENS FOSTER

RESILIENCE

*An ability to recover from or adjust easily to misfortune
or change. (https://www.merriam-webbster.com)*

The old oak tree welcomed the convertible with outstretched limbs. The sound of breaking glass and twisted metal echoed across Lake Nokomis, filling the air with the sound and fury of the wreckage. The sight of the accident revealed that the passenger and driver were alive because the convertible had enough space for the impact to move their bodies backward when the front end of the car was pushed into the front seat. Pictures of the car in the *Star Tribune* September 21, 1964 (Sandy's 24th birthday), made a person gasp and wonder how the occupants had lived through the accident. The passenger was conscious but Sandy was unconscious when they were extracted from the car.

Our parents were at his side two days later when Sandy regained consciousness. His first visual awareness was of Judge and Coach Warmath at his bedside. Then he heard Mom crying quietly in the background, being comforted by Dad. (It hurt my heart to stay in Uniontown instead of going with our parents to Minnesota. I had quit my job in D.C. and rushed home only to be instructed to stay there to manage the funeral home affairs and keep an eye on the twins until our parents returned home. Thank God he survived the ordeal.)

As soon as he woke up, Sandy tried to assure everyone in the room that he was okay. When reality set in, he started to assess his situation. He could see and feel some obvious injuries--a cast on his left arm and a foot-to-knee cast on his right leg. He remembered ankle pain from the break he had suffered on his right leg in his junior year in high school. He remained wary of being hit on the broken ribs he sustained in a game on his 21st birthday. However, those mishaps did not compare to the level of pain he was experiencing this time. He knew what he could see was the tip of the iceberg.

Sandy sustained more injuries than the press

reported, but fewer than the doctors found when they performed exploratory surgery. He had broken ribs and some bruising of organs, but miraculously no internal organs sustained major damage. He was thrilled to get that information. The piece of news that spoke to and could have shaken his spirit was the medical opinion that his mobility would be limited and his ability to run or participate in sports again was highly unlikely.

Such a prognosis could have been devastating, but Sandy Stephens' attitude did not allow him to accept the opinions of the doctors as his truth. He called on the basic tenets ingrained in his psyche by the tutelage of others and personal experience. He prayed for God's help in every phase of the recovery process ahead of him and, as usual, envisioned the best possible outcome. But first he had to get to the rehab stage.

A hospital stay is traumatic on many levels, not the least of which are the indignities a person must endure as a patient. Being embarrassed was never appealing to Sandy, but for such a proud man, the realities involved in being bedridden sent embarrassment to another level and added to his pain. He was immobilized and forced to accept assistance with his basic

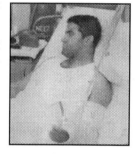

physical needs. It took a while for Sandy to accept that nurses are equipped to help their patients overcome their concerns about modesty by treating them with care and professionalism. The necessity for such assistance stretched his dignity to limits beyond his worst nightmare. I believe the situation gave him the incentive to heal and get out of that bed much faster than the doctors could predict.

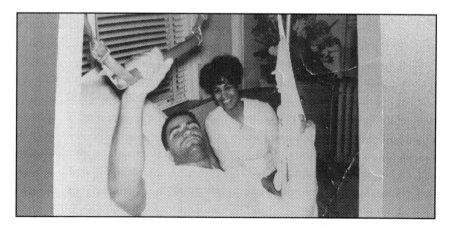

Sandy's foot and elbow were reconstructed. Healing both limbs couldn't take place in earnest until his ribs healed and the casts were removed. (One of the pins inserted in his reconstructed elbow in 1964 was still in him when he passed away in 2000.) Sandy followed the rehabilitation protocols suggested by the doctors when he finally emerged from the hospital, but he went beyond their programming because he believed he would walk, run, and return to a level of athleticism that would be limited only by his ability to get an opportunity to perform.

There are many articles about Sandy that reference his accident. None that I found report his resolve to rebound from his injuries and the steps he took to persevere through his rehabilitation. His frame of mind during everything he endured, in and out of the hospital, amazed those who knew him.

Even while in the burn unit, there was never an expressed complaint [by Sandy]. (M. Hudson––MN Friend)

It was very impressive to see Sandy come back and after having a serious auto accident; many thought he wouldn't. (J. Williams (deceased) ––Friend/Legacy Supporter)

Sandy's spirit was strong and undeniable even after what was considered disabling injuries. He worked until he could once again play world-class football (S. Allen––Cousin)

Sandy not only regained the use of his right foot and left arm, he went on to play football in the National Football League (NFL) on the taxi squad of the Kansas City Chiefs in 1966.

After being told I would never walk properly again, I joined the Kansas City Chiefs one and a half years later. I started as running back but got a chance to play QB by playing opposing QB against the No. 1 defense of the Chiefs. After two years of frustration, I decided I would never get a real opportunity, so I finally gave up the fight. It was the end of my football career––no regrets––I had a storybook collegiate career! **Sandy Stephens**

The NFL quest was over, the promised land unreached. But Sandy's thirst to excel in athletic contests never changed. Tennis, racquetball, handball, and finally golf became his new passions. He brought his fierce competitive spirit to each sport.

Those who have a competitive spirit are enthusiastic about the competition and often they seek this type of competitive atmosphere in whatever they do. These people are often seen as being very confident and always up to a challenge. (Bayt.com)

Sandy was one of the most competitive guys I know. He and I were constantly competing in something. Whether it was cerebral games like chess, checkers, or backgammon, or physical games, such as racquetball, every point was contested and neither of us would give the other the benefit of the call. He was always prepared and persevered in whatever the game was. (M. Harrison––Friend/Program Director)

To this day I know I was a better golfer than Sandy and he knew it too, however, I could never beat him. He even told me, "I know you could beat me, but I'm not going to let you." He just had that mental toughness and "dirt" that would always enable him to pull off a victory. The kind of will we see today in Tiger Woods and Serena Williams, as examples. (O. Courtney––MN Brother-Friend)

PAY IT FORWARD

Respond to a person's kindness to oneself by being kind to someone else.
(dictionary.com)

MENTORSHIP

One of the positions Sandy held in 1978 was Vice President and General Manager for the JLH Corporation. The corporation offered a "Professional Football Camp for Youngsters 8 to 18" at Allen University and Benedict College in Columbia, South Carolina. An excerpt from the brochure that was sent to parents by the company president, James L. Harold, stated:

Dear Parent,

We've organized the J.L.H. Professional Football Camp as a learning experience for young athletes. Our goals are to assist in the development of the total athlete through sports, in this case football. We feel that our camp participants will not only improve measurably as football players, but they will also learn the value of discipline and hard work. We believe that their camp experience will develop the personal characteristics of sportsmanship, cooperation, understanding, initiative and self-reliance, which will make them more complete individuals. Our philosophy is predicated on the concept that constructive athletic competition is a teaching device, the rewards of which reach far beyond the playing field.

The campers received guidance and skills training from coaches at the high school, college, and professional football levels. Several of the award-winning athletes who joined Sandy at the camp were Walter Payton (Chicago Bears), Stu Voight (Minnesota Vikings), Donnie Shell (Pittsburgh Steelers), Rickie Harris (Buffalo Bills), and Tim Baylor (Baltimore Colts).

In addition to mentoring youth, Sandy sought ways to help other athletes learn from his experiences––positive or challenging. He and a friend developed a proposal to provide career guidance and consulting services for young people who aspired to athletic success. Many of them needed to be given practical information and tutorials about the obstacles they could face in their efforts to reach their professional goals. The men's efforts did not culminate in a thriving enterprise but they represent an example of the types of visionary enterprises Sandy put into practice. Involvement in this type of entrepreneurship was how Sandy spent much of his energy after his playing days. If an opportunity to mentor young people was the goal, he was passionate about finding a way to take a talking point from an idea to a reality.

GIVING BACK

Supporting organizations that fought against the unfortunate cultural norms mentioned earlier was Sandy's desire. The organizations he admired offered programs designed to make a positive impact on the physical, intellectual, and emotional growth of young people. Several of his positions involved working with and for young people, whether serving as a coach or partnering with organizations to expose youth to sporting events, concerts, and other horizon-expanding activities.

Annually, Sandy spent his summers serving as a celebrity attraction where the proceeds benefited youth programs and scholarships. He left a treasure trove of calendars that show the depth of his commitment to share his reputation, athleticism, and personality for worthy causes. He kept track of his activities and commitments on handwritten calendars. A representative snapshot can be found in 1994. The events included:

- ➤ January – Community of Unity Celebration; Pro Sports Banquet
- ➤ February – Black & Gold Charity Ball (A Φ A)
- ➤ April – Celebrity Roast – Lou Grossman Foundation; U of M Spring Game – Commentator/Coach
- ➤ May – Ray Christensen Roast – U of M Children's Foundation
- ➤ June – Windows & Mirrors – Edgerton Elem. School – Speaker; Celebrity Classic – SW State Univ.; NFL Alumni Golf
- ➤ July – Twin City Football & Life Camp – Larry Cylkowski;
- ➤ 2nd Chance for Life Foundation Golf – Cal Stoll; United Parcel Celebrity Golf – Arthritis Foundation; Celebrity Golf Classic – John Autry; Celebrating Community (NFLAA)

- ➤ August – Rose Bowl Hall of Fame Induction; Celebrity Best Ball Golf – Isanti Sheriff's Dept; Ataxia Attack Golf -Bob Allison/Steve Hurvitz; Adith Miller Classic Golf; Inner City Golf Tournament – Professional Sports Linkage
- ➤ September – Murray Warmath Scholarship Night; Celebrity Golf – Ronald McDonald – Waconia
- ➤ November – Gopher Sports Hall of Fame Induction
- ➤ December – Sports Legends Weekend; Murray Warmath Birthday Party

Other calendar entries Sandy made included reminders about birthdays, graduations, anniversaries, interviews, speaking engagements at churches and community organizations, and appearances for U of MN events.

In a commentary about his community involvement Sandy noted:

> Although I participate in many community events sponsored by the NFL Alumni Association, Sports Legends, and the University of Minnesota "M" Club, I particularly enjoy playing in celebrity golf tournaments put on for the benefit of charitable organizations, e.g., the Special Olympics, Courage Center, Big Brothers & Big Sisters, and others.

The information for Joe Schmidt's golf tournament, which annually kicked off Sandy's calendar of charitable events for the summer, was in front of his other commitments when Sandy passed away in June 2000. He was ready to continue giving back in the way he loved.

SCHOLARSHIPS

Gopher men represent an embarrassment of riches regarding their intelligence, determination, perseverance, athletic prowess, camaraderie, community service, humanity, and titles. One of the best newspaper articles I read about Gopher football, "Inseparable," was written by Dennis Brackin, *Star Tribune* staff writer. The article commemorated the Gopher Football National Championship, 40th Anniversary––1960–2000. In the article, Sandy's brother-friend Judge (Dickson) called Stephens and Warmath "inseparable for reasons that extended far beyond football."

Shortly before he passed away, Sandy envisioned an event to recognize Coach Warmath's contribution to the University of Minnesota and Gopher football. He shared his idea with Judge, who **carried the ball** to complete the **play**––as he had done so many times throughout their friendship. Judge's unshakable devotion to his friend and his coach resulted in the development of special recognitions for Sandy and Coach Warmath.

For Sandy he spearheaded a group of Gopher greats and supporters that included McKinley Boston, the late John M. Williams, Bobby Bell–– HOF '83, Carl Eller––HOF '04, Miles Cohen, and Tom Moe. The group worked tirelessly to convince U of MN athletic department officials that Sandy's contributions to the athletic reputation of the institution deserved recognition by retiring his jersey. They persevered and were victorious. Our family is indebted to these champions. (Sandy's number [15] is still worn by Gopher men.)

Simultaneous with this initiative, the group was expanded to commence fundraising efforts for the development of a Sandy Stephens Endowed Scholarship. The scholarship is "given each year to a deserving African-American student-athlete in the university's football program who has demonstrated leadership, courage, and a commitment to civic and community responsibilities."[2] (Big Ten Conference 2008) Judge adds, "I, as well as others, mentor the individuals who have received this scholarship. Each of them is a tremendous young man. They conduct themselves as gentlemen, and those are the things that Sandy represented and the success in those areas keeps the essence of Sandy alive."[3] (Big Ten Conference 2008) The men who have received the scholarship are Dominique Sims, Amir Pinnix, Derrick Wells, Garrett Brown, Ryan Orton, MarQueis Gray, Jerry Gibson, and Nolan Edmonds.

Personal testimonies of the first recipients of the Sandy Stephens Endowed Scholarship show Sandy's importance from their point of view.

❖ In response to the survey question, "How do you believe Sandy contributed to the fight for equal opportunity for athletes in the United States?", Dominique Sims responded:

He pioneered it! He proved it in his living example. His actions were the beginning of his major contribution. His follow-through was his character as a man. (D. Sims––U of MN Endowed Scholarship Recipient)

❖ An excerpt from an article highlighting Amir Pinnix' accomplishments included his praise of the legendary athletes he admired, including Sandy:

"Being a student-athlete gave me a platform to do so and make a difference in my community. Those before me, such as Sandy Stephens, Jim Brown, Muhammad Ali, Paul Robeson, Bill Russell, Bobby Bell, Alan Page, and many others, were not only known for their greatness on the athletic field. They were also known for standing up for civil rights and what they believed in. They were my role models; they are Black history to me." Amir Pinnix, Gophersports.com 2/6/17

Sandy also influenced the development of high school students and younger athletes when he became a member and consultant for the Sports Legends Program in Newark, New Jersey.

An important part of the Sports Legends' activities was visiting local schools. The Legends entertained and enlightened students with stories of their lives and athletic exploits. They delivered their messages in the context of personal experiences to give the youngsters a glimpse of the paths they had traveled and how well they understood some of the seemingly insurmountable obstacles life can present. The Legends emphasized the importance of the students staying in school, remaining drug free, and having a vision for success. The youths may have heard the same messages from other adults in their lives but hearing how well-known sports men and women overcame tough situations on their way to success was inspiring for everyone who attended their sessions.

After his death in 2000, Sandy's daughter, son-in-law, niece, and I were invited to represent him at the annual November Sports Legends weekend. Milton Harrison, the Sports Legends Director and friend, was a gracious host who treated us like royalty. It was fun being able to introduce the younger family members to dear friends and iconic athletes such as Jim Marshall, Bobby Bell, Oscar Reed, Carl Eller, John Gilliam, Tim Baylor, Lou Hudson, and Gene Washington. We were thrilled to meet other Sports Legends such as, Tony Oliva, John Thomas, Norman Tate, Steve Braun, Ben Davidson, Randall McDaniel, Jerry Harkness, Marv Fleming, and many more.

Over the course of the weekend we learned about the athletes' extraordinary accomplishments and backgrounds. They appreciated Sandy's contributions to the world of sport and shared many heartfelt as well as funny stories about their interactions with him. I felt as if they adopted us as their family and took care of us in special, caring ways.

The Sports Legends set up a scholarship in Sandy's name. The criteria required candidates to be well-rounded high school student athletes who excelled in the classroom and community service as well as sports activities. We enjoyed meeting the first honoree and his mother at the Legends' banquet. They were grateful for the scholarship and the positive qualities Sandy represented. The Sports Legends and the student-athlete had a great time interacting with each other throughout the evening.

Although the Sports Legends program no longer exists, the former director notes:

There were a lot of kids that were touched by the program, and many college scholarships were given out as a result of the program. (M. Harrison––Friend/Program Director)

Sandy continued to share his fraternal spirit through his positive, caring attitude toward the many lives he touched as a participant in NFL Alumni Association projects, causes, and events.

GENEROSITY

Liberality in spirit or act characterized by a noble or forbearing spirit.
(Source unknown)

Generosity can be discussed and modeled, but I believe a person must be born with a noble or forbearing spirit to live a life of generosity. Sandy was an excellent example of a generous person. Many of the unscripted responses on the surveys speak to Sandy's inherent generous way of being. Here are some examples:

He was [also] a very generous person with his time, especially as it related to helping the less fortunate, especially young people. (O. Courtney—MN Brother-Friend)

Sandy had a way about himself of making everyone included and gave one hope. When he talked with you, he made you feel that you were very important. (J. Williams (deceased)—Friend/Supporter)

His friendship and loyalty, his generous nature, and willingness to share whatever he had. (M. Hickenbottom—Lifelong Friend)

He was always ready to help his friends. He might not agree with their actions, but he was there for them. And on Mother's Day, he always sent me a card, expressing his love. (A. McLee—Extended Family)

He was so caring and willing to share with others, emotionally and financially. (C. McLee—Uniontown Brother-Friend)

Friends were important to him. Sandy was one of the most caring and thoughtful people I know. He is the only good friend I know and have that I could always count on receiving a birthday card and a Christmas card [from]. Guys simply do not do that. (M. Harrison—Friend/Program Director)

I would never have met my husband had it not been for Sandy. He and I drove together to Bill Munsey's wedding. Sandy drove me all the way back home when I looked on my finger and noticed my ring, with much sentimental value, was missing. Sandy never gave it a second thought about taking me back to look for it. He knew how much it meant and how concerned I was that it was missing. I did find my ring and we got back before the wedding started. (M. Hudson––MN Friend)

As a superstar quarterback at the University of Minnesota he took time to write letters, send photos, and think of a young star struck cousin. As a result of his confidence, self-assurance, and humanity Sandy was one of the lynchpins of my strong, caring family upbringing that has helped me survive and flourish in a very diversified life and world. (S. Allen––Cousin)

His honesty, how he viewed life and trusted life. He wanted to always be fair and helpful. I admired his strength and love of people no matter how he might have been used or abused. He was a pillar of strength and humility at the same time. (T. Hitchcock––Marathoner/Writer/Friend)

Sandy was delighted to accept an invitation in 1985 from the Homecoming Executive Committee:

Dear Mr. Stephens: This fall the Golden Gopher football team will be generating a lot of excitement and high expectations, reminiscent of 1960-61 when the U of M won the Rose Bowl. To bring back some of the flavor of a truly fantastic football season, we are asking you to be a participant in the 1985 University of Minnesota Homecoming Parade. Having you present to celebrate the 25th Anniversary of the Gopher Rose Bowl win would surely be one of the highlights of this year's Homecoming.

Nothing made Sandy happier than to be invited to speak to the men on the Gopher Football Team. He and his teammates could inspire hope and determination in ways others could not because they had experienced going from a team with the worst record in the Big Ten to the 1960 Big Ten Co-Champions, the 1960 National Champions, and in 1962 the ultimate Rose Bowl triumph. Then Gopher Head Coach Lou Holtz thanked Sandy for the letter of encouragement he sent to the team in 1985.

Coach Tim Brewster and Governor Arne Carlson invited Sandy to join the Gopher football team when they visited the Governor's mansion. The invitation gave Sandy the opportunity to interact with the players in a relaxed, fun atmosphere.

I accompanied Sandy to one of the Governor's luncheons. Several players expressed to me how much they revered Sandy and enjoyed meeting him personally. Everyone would have benefited if there had been more opportunities for Sandy to share his enthusiasm and love for Gopher Sports with young players.

Sandy's giving ways fell closer to home when he showed extraordinary generosity and determination to make sure I was able to get home from school for the holidays:

Sandy graciously agreed to pick me up from Penn State for Christmas break my sophomore year. I invited a fellow student who lived close to Uniontown to ride with us. We were two of the few students still waiting to go home hours after other students had taken off in cars and buses. Making matters worse, the light snow of a few hours earlier had turned into a major snowstorm. When I called home to find out when to expect Sandy, Mom said he and his wife should have arrived long before my phone call.

Penn State is located on Nittany Mountain in the center of Pennsylvania and in 1962 a drive up the mountain on a two-lane highway was required to get to it. Winter in PA (prior to the development of winter tires) meant every sensible driver in PA had chains in the trunk of their car to help with tire traction when driving conditions became treacherous.

While I was calling home, Sandy, who had put chains on his tires when the weather started getting bad, was halfway up the mountain dealing with a broken chain link. The broken chain had to be removed to avoid getting it wrapped around the wheel axle. All this activity was going on in the snow, in the cold. I was very happy to see him when he finally arrived, but we knew we didn't have time for a long reunion because we needed to get back down the mountain. The tire chain was repaired and away we went.

The storm had become a blizzard by the time we arrived at the Pennsylvania Turnpike. The scene was unbelievable. The people who left school hours before us were among the hundreds of travelers in cars, trucks, and buses immobilized by at least a foot of wind-whipped snow and stranded on the road above the Midway Service Plaza. Luckily, we didn't need gas because there was no way to get to the pumps. Most people would have been satisfied to wait until plows arrived, but Sandy Stephens was not most people.

When Sandy saw a big rig start making its way through the crowd, he followed close behind. The Turnpike was closed to all traffic, so the truck crossed the median and barreled down the wrong side of the road with Sandy's convertible and his passengers close behind. We were traveling east on a more passable roadbed away from the storm. The Midway Plaza is more than 100 miles away from Uniontown, but at least we were moving. It wouldn't be long now. Then the chain on the rear tire on the driver's side broke and this time it wrapped around the axle. It had to be removed if the car was going to move.

We were able to pull over, but the shoulder of the road was narrow. That fact is pertinent because in order to remove the chain, Sandy had to get down on the ground on the driver's side of the car. His car had a detachable light in the trunk, so I got out of the car to help him see what he was doing and to wave off the few trucks that passed so they wouldn't run over his legs. Of course, he kept telling me to get back inside because it was bitterly cold, but I was more prepared for the weather than he was. His sense of style didn't include wearing winter boots and a heavy overcoat. I knew his leather jacket and lightweight slacks were no match for the "hawk."

I pointed out to my brother that he couldn't remove the chain and hold the light at the same time, so, like it or not, I was staying with him. This time I won the stubborn battle. It wasn't a smart time to argue and he was miserable, but his pride kept him from showing anything other than strength. I felt bad for him, his wife, and my friend. They wouldn't have been in this mess if it weren't for me. The sooner we could take care of the problem the better. With teamwork we managed to solve our dilemma and get home the next morning. My friend's parents picked her up and I promptly fell asleep with my arms wrapped around my nephew, Sanford III, the newest addition to the Stephens family. **Barbara R. Stephens Foster**

Sandy never mentioned the dismal conditions we experienced and the discomfort he felt. The trip was a prime example of the depth of his love for me, his generous spirit, and his determination to get us home in one piece.

Chapter 5

REFLECTIONS

MINNSYLVANIANS

Most of this book is devoted to the years we have spent in Minnesota. Sandy was the reason we were drawn here. We became Minnsylvanians in large measure because Mom fell in love with the Twin Cities when she and Dad attended some Gopher games in 1959 and 1960 and again for Sandy's wedding in 1961. When Ray and Joyce decided to attend the University of Minnesota, the decision to move was made.

PapPap decided to return to his roots in Pittsburgh when the Stephens clan moved to Minnesota. He did not believe Minnesota's climate was conducive to continuing his habit of taking a daily walk. The 80-year-old patriarch returned to Pittsburgh to live with Aunt Betty and our cousins. We went back to visit him when we could and finally to say goodbye when PapPap passed away in 1968 the same way he had lived––quietly. We commemorated his life with abiding love, a toast of bourbon, and peals of laughter as he and his pipe went to his eternal rest.

Mom, Raymond, and Joyce arrived in Minnesota in 1965 immediately after the twins' high school graduation. Sandy, his wife, and son had returned to Minnesota after living in Canada where he played professional football. By the summer of 1965 four of the six Stephens family members resided in Minnesota. In August 1965 Dad completed the sale of the funeral home, drove to Minnesota, and suffered a massive stroke several days after his arrival. His condition compelled Mom to request that I resign my position in Washington and join the family in the Twin Cities.

The University of Minnesota was the logical place to look for a job because the Minneapolis campus was within walking distance of our apartment. I applied for several positions and accepted one offered by the General College (GC). The GC Dean's office became my home away from home for the next three decades. So began my Minnesota reputation as Sandy Stephens' sister. Our personal identities here were originally based on our connection to him. It took about seven years for people to realize my name was Barbara. Then and now, all we need to do is mention our connection to Sandy and people immediately start regaling us with stories of their Gopher football memories and his place in them.

During their short residency in Minnesota our parents made an indelible impression on the community. Dad recuperated from his stroke and was credentialed as an embalmer in Minnesota––with limited use of his left hand. He went to work as a receptionist for Pilot City where he was recognized as an outstanding employee. He also was a caretaker for a men's shelter and a revered member of the Minnesota chapter of the B.P.O. of ELKS Lodge after he transferred his membership from PA. Mom used her former experience as a social worker to join the Hennepin County Welfare Department after Dad recovered. She won the hearts of her clients and all our friends.

The Stephens family is split evenly between the states when it comes to marriage––Mom, Dad, and Joyce wed in PA, and Sandy, Raymond, and I wed in MN. Our children are all Minnesotans who claim a strong attachment to PA, particularly Uniontown and the surrounding area. When Stephens family members pass away, services are held first in Minnesota then in Pennsylvania. We are laid to rest with our maternal grandparents, aunts, and uncles.

One of the situations I find ironic is that Dad, the master embalmer and funeral director, could not be embalmed due to the circumstances of his passing. He was the first family member to be cremated to permit the interment of his remains next to his beloved wife. After the memorial service in Minnesota we drove to Pennsylvania and conducted our dad's memorial service in the sanctuary of City Chapel, the church Dad sold the building to before leaving PA.

The church's sanctuary was formerly the chapel of the Stephens Funeral Home. Friends and family came in large numbers to show their support and give us comfort. It was a lovely, remarkably poignant service filled with equal amounts of joy and sorrow and a fitting farewell for Dad and his spirit. The full impact of our loss hit me as I carried the container that held Dad's ashes across the front porch of the church/house. At that moment, one of the two instances of hysterical crying I have experienced in my life hit me. Such a reaction was startling to everyone, especially me. Sandy wrapped his arm around my shoulders and I could not move. Being immobilized was a problem since I wanted to walk around the house and let the memories wash over me. After I collected myself and Sandy was convinced the worst had passed, he let me go. A friend and I took a stroll into the backyard and my spirit quieted,

Several years after Dad's service, my son Lee, and our cousin George, a.k.a. Chip, were blessed in the church. We felt an affinity for City Chapel because the pastor had baptized us at Mount Rose Baptist Church years before. The church subsequently purchased the property next to our former home to build a new church, and our former home was returned to its original layout as a duplex to provide revenue for the congregation. There will not be any other ceremonies held in the house, but when we visit Uniontown, I find joy sharing family stories about the homestead with my grandchildren, nieces, and nephews.

During the past fifty-four years, all of us have found a way to build on the Stephens legacy of spirituality, athleticism, musicality, education, and community service. In MN, as we were in PA, we have been blessed with a group of friends and colleagues who are stellar human beings. They inspire, comfort, prod, support, challenge, love, and make us laugh when we need it.

Sandy was interviewed for an article in The Twin Cities Courier titled, "Former Gopher still loves Minnesota best." The article includes quotes about Minnesota from Sandy: "But I always had to come back to Minnesota," he said. "It's still the greatest place I've found in all the United States." Another: "I want to give something back to Minnesota because the state has been so good to me," As a family, we will continue to share our hearts equally between Pennsylvania and Minnesota and say our final farewells in both places.

LEGACY

Something that someone has achieved that continues to exist
after they stop working or die.
(https://www.macmillandictionary.com)

Sandy Stephens was an extraordinarily complex individual whose interests far exceeded his accomplishments as an athletic trail blazer, tenacious opponent, and fierce competitor in the sports arenas where he left his mark. He was propelled from the playgrounds of Uniontown, PA, to national prominence to community contributor. He loved with ardor, laughed with abandon, and sang like a hit maker. He always expected to be the best, and although life did not always go according to his plan, he never faltered in his pursuit of love, justice, and joy.

He starred in many roles——son, brother, friend, father, grandfather, godfather, sportsman, music lover, fraternity brother, spiritual truth examiner, entrepreneur, and fun-loving gentleman——to name a few. He walked through life armed with undeniable gifts and talents imbued in his psyche and manifested through practice. His daughter and friends share their perspectives here.

I am proud that my children and grandchildren have an honorable legacy to carry on. It should inspire them to not only dream, but to succeed in every aspect of their lives. (J. Gloster——Daughter)

He was just a very honest person who believed that he could make a difference and leave his legacy that people who knew him or of him could grow from his examples. (T. Hitchcock——Marathoner/Writer/Friend)

Funny, approachable, business minded, used common sense. I've not heard anyone say they would like to avoid Sandy—— except for defenses. (D. Pothier——MN Brother-Friend/Mentor)

Sandy's family and friends have been a phenomenal support for me, and I know I am part of the Stephens family! (D. Sims—Sandy Stephens Endowed Scholarship Recipient)

He ASPIRED, to INSPIRE, before he EXPIRED. (C. McLee—Uniontown Brother-Friend)

An excerpt from "The Golden Leader" article on the Big Ten Official Athletic Site, February 18, 2008, includes:

At the end of his collegiate career, Stephens had cemented himself into Minnesota football history. He was the first African American quarterback in school history. He led the Gophers to their sixth national championship, and their first since 1941. He was instrumental in taking Minnesota to back-to-back Rose Bowl trips and is still the only quarterback in Gopher history to lead a team to the Tournament of Roses. These are glimpses of what was remembered about Stephens' career, but most important in the eyes of former teammates and friends, he will be remembered as simply a leader. [1]

Stephens family members have been avid fans of Sandy with good reason. Our cousin shared this observation of a contribution Sandy made to quarterback posterity. I wonder how many others are aware of this part of his legacy:

Let us not forget a movement that Sandy brought to the American football scene . . . the lifting of the left foot to put a man in motion. Although at the time many of the "expert pundits of the day" stated he was giving away his intentions. Is there a quarterback today that does not use this movement? (S. Allen—Cousin)

Coach Warmath and I became buddies by attending various athletic competitions, alumni events, and college recognitions at the U of MN. A particularly fun day was when we participated in passing a football, person by person, from the Metrodome to the groundbreaking site for the new TCF Bank Stadium on campus.

I passed the ball to a 12-year-old boy who noticed the signs my daughter Sharla, granddaughter Caprice, and I were holding. The young man said he was a Sandy Stephens fan. We talked for a while and I realized after a few minutes that he put my knowledge of Sandy's athletic career to shame. Although he was too young to have seen Sandy play, this youngster knew all Sandy's statistics at every position and the recognition he had received. I cried when the young man told me he considered Sandy the greatest football player in Minnesota history. His knowledge and praise would have made Sandy burst with happiness. His dream to be remembered by future generations was manifested in front of my eyes.

It was a beautiful Minnesota day charged with the same energy we felt as fans walking to Memorial Stadium to watch the Gophers play in the glory days. Everyone was cheering and clapping as we passed the ball. Then, we followed the ball along the route to the new site. The signs Sharla, Caprice, and I were carrying recognized the Stephens quarterbacks: Sandy, #15, Rose Bowl/Big Ten/National champ and Ray, #12, Big Ten champ. Both men contributed to the glory and history of Golden Gopher football.

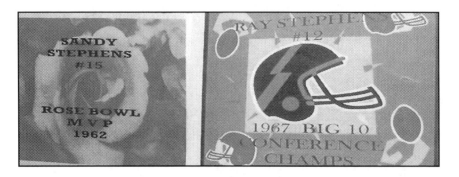

Many people in the crowd stopped us to share their memories of watching the Stephens brothers play ball. I felt Sandy's spirit beam with happiness at the ceremony. He was never willing to accept the loss of Gopher football on campus. Memorial Stadium represented the heart and soul of his university experience. The new landscape where the University Alumni Association building was built, while impressive, just wasn't the same.

On the historic groundbreaking day, and each time I saw Coach Warmath in the years after Sandy's death, we greeted each other warmly, commented about the current state of the football program, then cried together as we reminisced about how much we missed and loved Sandy.

SELECTED HALLS OF FAME MEMORIES

ROSE BOWL HALL OF FAME

Sandy was inducted into the **Rose Bowl Hall of Fame** in **1997**. Coach Pat Donahue shared the following introductory remarks about him:

Minnesota came West again, looking for redemption and a chance to get rid of some bitter memories. Stephens provided the spirit and energy and this time the Gophers, and Coach Murray Warmath, celebrated a methodical, 21-3 win over UCLA. Stephens completed 7 of 11 passes, scored two touchdowns, ran for 46 yards, and kept the Bruins in the dark with adept ball handling. The Gopher defense played its part by holding the Bruins to 45 yards rushing. Stephens was named player of the game and Coach Warmath called the win the most gratifying victory.

Sandy's remarks:

Thanks to my main cheerleaders over the years, my sisters, Barbara and Joyce, who are right down in front here. Stand up and please take a bow. Like most players, I take my cheerleaders with me and they've been with me over the years. But they shared my dreams early and that was to come here to this great stadium. When I was a youngster, I planned on getting here. I never dreamt about this day, though. This is icing on the cake. I would also like to thank some of the great teams that I played for in the 1961 and 1962 Rose Bowls. I would like to thank them for making it possible for me to be here. And most of all I'd like to thank my great coach, Murray Warmath, who made it possible, at a time when it wasn't favorable, to play a quarterback such as myself. He had belief in me and let me play and I fulfilled that opportunity and I'm here today.

WESTERN CHAPTER
PENNSYLVANIA SPORTS HALL OF FAME

The Stephens family faced a dilemma when Sandy was inducted into the **Western Pennsylvania Sports Hall of Fame (WPSHOF), May 1, 1999**. Sandy and Joyce's daughter Tiffany were being recognized simultaneously in different parts of the country. Tiffany was receiving her MBA (Master of Business Administration) from Florida A & M University (FAMU) while Sandy was scheduled for induction into the WPSHOF. If we did not attend his induction, it would be a family first. Sandy insisted we keep our plans to go to Florida and applaud Tiffany's accomplishments. Meanwhile Sandy's lifelong brother-friends in Uniontown were excited for the opportunity to step in and give Sandy the love and support he deserved for receiving the WPSHOF recognition. Pictured with Sandy are Lawrence Curry, Kenneth Finney (deceased), Richard Curry, John Moorman, Charles McLee, Richard Thomas, and Ozzie Minor (deceased). Sandy also had a chance to reconnect with Coach Bill Powers who joined him in the 1999 class of inductees.

FAYETTE COUNTY HALL OF FAME

On **July 18, 2009,** Sandy was posthumously inducted into the **Inaugural Fayette County Hall of Fame**. His daughter Jocelyn, son-in-law Terry, grandson Shane, grandniece Caprice, and I represented the family at the ceremony.

My remarks to the group included:

Sandy went on to achieve national acclaim as the first Black All-American quarterback at a major university. He is a member of the Rose Bowl Hall of Fame, the MN Sports Hall of Fame, the Gopher Sports Hall of Fame and the Western Pennsylvania Sports Hall of Fame. What would it mean to Sandy to be inducted into the first Fayette County Hall of Fame? All the pain he experienced 50 years ago would be washed away. He would be gratified to know that the people who knew and loved him first were publicly commending him for his athletic excellence and personal perseverance. This award and recognition would make his heart swell with pride and satisfaction. His spirit is doing the back flips he learned from Coach Everhart at Lafayette. **Barbara R. Stephens Foster**

Lesson learned: Injustices occur in life but deserved and often delayed accolades can heal!

PENNSYLVANIA SPORTS HALL OF FAME

Sandy was posthumously inducted into the **Pennsylvania Sports Hall of Fame** in **2010**. The Fayette County Hall of Fame chapter was represented by George Von Benko who joined Joyce, my son Lee and me in accepting the award.

My remarks to the group were:

Nothing would be more satisfying tonight than to have Sandy here to receive this award personally. In his absence, I offer the following snapshot of Sanford Stephens II, the man:

He was humble and proud, he was articulate and "down with it," he was handsome and reserved, he was a Christian and a spiritual truth seeker, he was fierce and unyielding, he was fastidious and compulsive, he was intense and mellow, he was sentimental and romantic, he was competitive and gracious, he was resourceful and visionary, he was funny and a jokester, he was loyal and patriotic, he was adored and loathed, he was respected and demeaned, he was generous and kind, he was a scholar and a teacher, he was a success and a failure, he was an eternal optimist with zero tolerance for injustice, he was bloodied and unbowed. Thank you for this honor,

---

COLLEGE FOOTBALL HALL OF FAME

Sandy was nominated for induction into the College Football Hall of Fame in 1990. The nomination letter was one of his prized possessions. Years later another nomination was submitted to the National Football Foundation. The nomination was approved and Sandy Stephens was posthumously inducted into the **National Football Foundation College Football Hall of Fame (CFHOF), December 6, 2011**, in New York City. Joining me at the final CFHOF events in South Bend, Indiana, were Joyce, Sandy's son Sanford III, my son Lee, my daughter Sharla, our cousin Stephen (Rice), and NFF supporter Hillary. At the time of his induction Sandy Stephens, the first Black All-American quarterback, joined an elite group of 1,094 inductees enshrined in the CFHOF. They represent less than .02% of the men who play or coach college football. Sandy's induction gives him a permanent place in the history of the sport, validation of his athletic excellence, and the conquest of his ultimate collegiate pinnacle of success.

Chapter 6

FAREWELLS

THE MAN WHO INSPIRED HOPE

Sandy interacted with teammates, fans and community members on many levels. He was known for his self-confidence, charm, intellect, and storytelling. His family and friends benefitted from all those attributes plus his love, compassion, and care. The nicknames he acquired from close friends as an adult were "Sweet Poppa," "El Poppa," and "the Poppa." He did not live long enough for me to probe into the genesis of the nickname, but I understand why it was perpetuated. He was the patriarch of the Stephens family after our parents passed away, so "Poppa" fit. He was blessed with a daughter, Jocelyn, and a son, Sandy III, who refer to him as "Pops." He was known as "Grandpa" to his grandchildren and great-grandchildren, most of whom did not get to know him personally, but they know of him from their parents, friends, and social media.

My letter to him at the end of these pages describes some of the things Minnesota family members loved and miss about Sandy. Many of his dearest friends have passed away, but others who still reside in the Twin Cities, Uniontown, and other parts of the country remain his stalwart supporters. Some of Sandy's friends who refer to him as "The Poppa" tell me they continue to commune with him daily. I never doubt them.

One of Sandy's lifelong friends who was introduced earlier is Bill Munsey. Bill acquired the nickname "Big Train" during his playing days to describe how he plowed through defensive lines. Bill was on a heart transplant list. Prior to Sandy's death Bill had visions of Sandy telling him to continue to pray and be hopeful. The two brother-friends had discussed what actions of respect they would show when one of them passed away. Because of Bill's condition, both men expected Sandy to be the one delivering his friend's eulogy. The opposite became the reality.

FUNERALS

It has been noted that Stephens family members have two funeral/memorial services. Bill's doctors gave him permission to travel to Minnesota but not to Uniontown for Sandy's wakes and funerals.

The wake for Sandy at Estes Funeral Home in Minneapolis drew a large crowd that included athletes, coaches, sports reporters, and fans. Thanks to our friend and Ray's teammate, Ezell Jones, the wake was professionally recorded. We have wonderful photos of many notable attendees greeting Coach Warmath, who was suffering at the loss of the young man he loved like a son.

Judge (Dickson) and Otis (Courtney surprised Coach Warmath with a framed, autographed picture of the 1960 championship team to lift his spirits. He was happy to recall those glory days. Bill Munsey, Carl Eller, Bob McNeil, Bobby Bell, John Robinson, and other Alpha Phi Alpha fraternity brothers held the organization's moving farewell ceremony. The entire experience was worthy of Sandy and what he meant to the community.

The funeral was held the next day at Pilgrim Baptist Church in Saint Paul. Once again, a large crowd, including high-level politicians, entertainers, and clergy gathered to pay homage to Sandy. I was in a daze and missed recognizing some of the people who were there, but the elements of the service I remember vividly are the on-point eulogy delivered by Rev. Robert L. Stephens. The title of the eulogy was "The

Option Player." Rev. Robert L. Stephens was not a relative and he did not know Sandy personally but he knew his athletic reputation. His words captured Sandy's ways of being in a passionate, knowledgeable manner. It was amazing.

The other memorable part of the funeral for me was hearing my daughter-friend Yolande Bruce deliver the selections we chose for the service. Yolande is a member of our extended family who put her own sadness aside to provide us with the solace only extraordinary music could provide.

Reverend Jesse L. Jackson Sr. was unable to attend Sandy's funeral in Minnesota. However, he expressed his condolences eloquently in a letter to me. Rev. Jackson wrote about the impact Sandy had on him personally, the NFL, and civil rights. Part of his compelling prose reads, "I am convinced his (Sandy's) dreams of having an even playing field for his skills to be demonstrated were broken, but his non-negotiable dignity and private pride was never broken."

The wake for Sandy in Uniontown was held in the chapel of Lantz' Funeral Home, the other Black funeral home referred to in Chapter 1. The Lantz' Funeral Home legacy has been perpetuated by passing the business down to family members. Despite the competitive nature of the businesses, there have been multiple intersections between our families for 70 years.

Family and friends of the four of us came to offer their condolences.

We were surrounded by people who knew and loved Joyce, Raymond, and me as much as they loved Sandy. I felt more comfort than sorrow. The funeral at our home church, Mt. Rose Baptist Church, was a less formal affair than the service in Minnesota. It was filled with storytelling about Sandy's exploits in Uniontown and the influence he had on the lives of the men and women who had loved and admired him. It reminded me of the high esteem Sandy held for iconic athletes: Charley Sifford and Tiger Woods––golf; Wilma Rudolph, Rafer Johnson, and Ralph Boston––track; Althea Gibson, Arthur Ashe, Venus and Serena Williams––tennis; and Wayne Embry––basketball GM. All their stories show how perseverance led them to be beacons of hope for generations to follow. Sandy's family and friends felt that he was worthy of joining such an elite group. There is no doubt his spirit rejoiced.

We have extraordinary friends who go to great lengths to care for us. The round trip from the church to the cemetery in PA takes up to three hours. When we returned to the church, we had a full-course hot meal waiting for us and many funeral attendees came back and joined us. We are blessed.

IN HIS WORDS

As we come to the end of this walk with Sandy Stephens, the Black Moses of quarterbacks, his reflections help us hear his joy when he witnessed the strides another man made as he followed in the footsteps of his predecessor and continued the journey to a triumphant end:

The first Grambling vs. Morgan State Classic I attended was in 1972, shortly after my arrival in New York City. I compared the game to the Rose Bowl, which I had the good fortune to play in twice. The players would have the same perspective my teammates and I had at the Rose Bowls——the knowledge that this would be the highlight of their season. They were playing in New York City, in Yankee Stadium, before 65,000+ fans, many of whom were Black fans from the entire Eastern seaboard. This had to be one of the finest settings anywhere for a performer of any nature.

Now that I had the pleasure of attending my second Classic, I was pulling for the highly touted quarterback, Doug Williams, who was being pushed by the major college polls as a candidate for the Heisman Trophy and All-America status. I wanted him to have his finest day ever in this setting. In my heart I felt his statistics were sound enough to make him a solid contender for the Heisman Trophy, but I was painfully aware of the loopholes and excuses others might be inclined to use against him in his quest to become a successful Black quarterback. I realized it was 15 years prior that the first Black man, my friend Ernie Davis, had won the award. Much of Doug's professional success would be determined by which team, and particularly which coach, he played under.

****

Years later, my heart soared when Doug Williams, the man who attained All-American status as a quarterback many years after me, took the position to Olympian heights by leading his team to win the coveted Super Bowl XXII in 1988. As an extra, added dimension, he was voted the MVP of the game. Now there was irrefutable evidence that a Black man had all the skills, tools, and instincts to be a champion in the NFL. He had reached the "Promised Land" of Black quarterback success.

We know that suffering produces perseverance; perseverance, character; and character, hope. (Romans 5:3-4, NIV Bible)

CLOSURE

A LETTER TO MY BIG BROTHER
(9/21/2019)

Dear Sandy,

As we approach the 79th anniversary of your birth, we are finally able to publish a tribute to your wisdom in a book and on social media via www.awalkwiththeblackmoses.com. You were a very special person who had visions of accomplishment and the determination to scale mountains to succeed. You had some success and some missteps but remained blessed throughout. Legions of people know of your athletic exploits.

Your grandchildren have inherited many plaques, trophies, citations, and pictures to commemorate your life. You were a marquee quarterback before the term was coined. You went to the Big Ten because teams in the Big Ten competed for the right to go to the Rose Bowl––the oldest bowl game with the finest reputation and biggest arena. You always wanted the biggest and the best for yourself and others.

The heady experience of attaining your Rose Bowl dream was lessened by Minnesota's loss to Washington in 1961. Through a quirk of fate–– God's sense of justice––you were given an opportunity to make it right. Those of us who know and love you were not surprised when you were named the MVP of the 1962 Rose Bowl Minnesota triumph over UCLA. No mere eleven opposing men could keep you from coming away with a "W" once you had a second chance at your cherished dream. You and your teammates were unbeatable that day. As their leader, you foretold the future and showed what the awesome, pioneering, godfather of Black quarterbacks, Sandy Stephens, represented. You were a legendary athlete who will always be noted in sports annals, but your athleticism isn't what we, your family and friends, miss about you.

We miss your caring ways, your "just checking up on you" phone calls; your birthday, get-well, sympathy, and thinking-of-you cards; your willingness to spearhead fundraising campaigns for friends in need; and your generous gifts. We miss your sense of humor––those sometimes hysterical, sometimes pitiful jokes and how you could find a silly joke so funny you would laugh until tears fell (especially when you and Bill Munsey were telling old war stories). We miss your ability to be fully engaged in one of your favorite table games––chess, backgammon, dominoes, or Millennium football––while simultaneously being tuned in to Solid Gold Soul on the stereo; reacting to a great play by the Chicago Cubs on one TV; cheering on the Vikings or Gophers on another TV; and switching channels to catch Tiger Woods' latest triumph.

Sandy, we miss watching you at family gatherings and challenging Ray to a heated game of backgammon to pass the time until we announced, "Dinner is served." We miss seeing you choose a recliner with a TV tray at your knee to enjoy the food––your leg pulsing up and down as a testament to the tastiness of the cuisine. Etched in our memory is the gleam in your eye at the first bite of Joyce's sweet potato pie. All was right with the world at that moment. The final holiday memory is of you leaning back in the recliner for "just a few minutes" to let your food settle before returning to "Sugar Hill" (your apartment) to fully relax and savor a piece of the personal sweet potato pie that was always baked for you. My pound cake would be included in the goodie bags (mini dinners) we always prepared for you and Ray to take home.

We miss your scowl when you disagreed with a point someone was trying to make in conversation; when you saw or heard of anyone being mistreated; when you expressed zero tolerance for your perception of stupidity; and when you pondered the mysteries of the universe. None of us wanted to be the target of your scowl if you were angry. There was never any doubt about why you were angry after you eloquently delivered your targeted message to the unfortunate recipient of your displeasure.

We miss coming to "Sugar Hill" to celebrate your birthdays or just to stop by (but never unannounced). You were always a gracious host, quick to offer some "pipe cooler" (liquid refreshment) and a snack from your food stores. I miss making you pots of spaghetti when you fell on hard times. The pots of spaghetti were replaced by large tubs of tuna salad in warm weather. The pots and tubs became symbols of our love, good times and bad, and the gesture did not cease until you passed away. You could make those food offerings last for a week with careful portioning. I miss giving you those small gifts.

We miss you recounting the back stories of your experiences in life and in athletics, especially life-changing occurrences in the seventh grade; facing racism and bigotry in the nation's capital; playing mediator between warring couples in the pros; and the beauty and wonder of the exotic places you visited in the world.

We will miss you forever.

Your loving sister,

Barbara

NOTES

INTRODUCTION

1   Butwin, David. 1959. "Sandy Stephens Day." *Minnesota DAILY.*

CHAPTER 1 – BEING STEPHENS

1   Von Benko, George. "Playgrounds played huge role in athletic successs." *HeraldStandard.com.* July 31, 2012 Accessed July 13, 2019. http://www. heraldstandard.com.

2   Jenkins, Sally. 2012. "Why Are Jim Thorpe's Olympc Records Stil Not Recognized?" Smithsonian Magazine, (The editors of Encyclopedia Britannica 2004)July 2012 Accessed July 2012. https://www.smithsonianmag.com.

3   The Official Licensing Website of Jackie Robinson, https://www.jackierobinson. com/biography

CHAPTER 2 – ADVERSITY

1   Connor, Marlene Kim. 2003. *What Is Cool? Understandung Black Manood in America.* Evanston: Agate.

2   The editors of Encyclopedia Britannica. 2004. "Fritz Pollard: American Football Player and Coah." *https://www.britannica.com.* July 16. Accessed July 13, 2019. https://www.britannica.com.

3   McDonald, Kwame. 2005. "Pollard finally inducted into NFL Hall of Fame. His case shows bigotry persists in college, pro sports." *MN Spokesman-Recorder, Kwame Kapsules,* August 11-17.

4   Bembry, Jerry. 2017. "George Taliaferro played quarterback and a whole lot more." *The Undefeated.* September 28. Accessed July 13, 2019. https:// theundefeated.com.

5   Bembry, Jerry. 2017. "George Taliaferro played quarterback and a whole lot more." *The Undefeated.* September 28. Accessed July 13, 2019. https:// theundefeated.com.

6   Reid, Jason. 2017. "Willie Thrower: A perfect name for a trailblazing quarterback." *The Undefeated,* October 5. Accessed July 13, 2019. https://theundefeated.com.

7   "Sandy Stephens Scaled his Everest" by Don Boxmeyer, Staff Writer

CHAPTER 3 – ROSE BOWL DREAM

1   Loftus, Charles. 1951. *What is a Football Player?* New Haven: College Football Hall of Fame.

2   Big Ten Conference. 2008. "The Golden Leader, Sandy Stephens - Minnesota Football." *Big Ten Official Athletic Site.* February 18. Accessed July 14, 2019. http://www.bigten.org.

3   https://www.thedailygopher.com/2016/12/29/14101400/minnesota-football-1962-rose-bowl-tbt/

The Daily Gopher

APPENDIX A

SURVEY QUESTION #1
What was your relationship with Sandy?

SURVEY QUESTION #2
Why did you value your relationship with Sandy?

SURVEY QUESTION #3
What personal attributes did Sandy exhibit that you admired?

SURVEY QUESTION #4
How do you believe Sandy contributed to the fight for equal opportunity for athletes in the United States?

SURVEY QUESTION #5
Were you affected personally by Sandy's athletic determination? If so, how?

SURVEY QUESTION #6
What four things should people know or remember about Sandy?

SURVEY QUESTION #7
What suggestions do you have for the title of a book about Sandy?

APPENDIX B

BASIC TOOLS FOR GREATNESS

- ➢ ASPIRATION – Directing one's hopes or ambitions toward achieving something.
- ➢ DETERMINATION – Firm or fixed intention to achieve a desired end.
- ➢ EDUCATION – The process of facilitating learning or the acquisition of knowledge, skills, values, beliefs, and habits.
- ➢ FAITH – To have faith is to be sure of the things we hope for, to be certain of the things we cannot see.
- ➢ GENEROSITY – Liberality in spirit or act characterized by a noble or forbearing spirit.
- ➢ INTELLIGENCE – The ability to learn or understand or to deal with new or trying situations: the ability to apply knowledge to manipulate one's environment.
  (https://www.merriam-webster.com)
- ➢ LEADERSHIP – The action of leading a group of people or an organization; creating an inspiring vision, and then motivating and inspiring others to reach that vision.
- ➢ MENTORSHIP – A relationship in which a more experienced or more knowledgeable person helps to guide a less experienced or less knowledgeable person.
- ➢ PERCEPTION – A way of regarding, understanding, or interpreting something; a mental impression.
- ➢ PERSEVERANCE – Continued effort to do or achieve something despite difficulties, failure, or opposition.
- ➢ PRIDE – The quality or state of being proud; a reasonable or justifiable self-respect; marked by stateliness, magnificence.

- ➢ RESILIENCE – An ability to recover from or adjust easily to misfortune or change.
- ➢ SENSE OF HUMOR – A personality that gives someone the ability to say funny things and see the funny side of things. (https://www.merriam-webster.com)

APPENDIX C

STATUS OF SANDY'S GOALS AND ASPIRATIONS

This book shares examples of the ways Sandy Stephens hoped, dreamed, and pursued goals and aspirations in his life. He was able to work his way up many mountains and he stumbled down into multiple valleys in pursuit of the lofty goals he set for himself. His hard work and perseverance resulted in more goals being met with success than disappointment.

Junior and Senior High School:

> Baseball trophies – pitching, home runs, triples, stolen bases, and base hits; switch hitter who could hit the ball 400 ft.; two professional baseball tryouts.
> Basketball medals – five medals in an eighth-grade basketball tournament including the MVP award.
> 3rd team All-State basketball team; conference leading scorer.
> Football – "Big 33" plaque as a member of the PA All-State team.
> Letterman – Uniontown Joint Senior High School – Three years each in football, basketball, and track.
> High point total in track during his county track meet.
> Multiple (50+) college offers, including West Point

Collegiate Recognitions:

> Quarterback at Division I school, University of Minnesota (1958 – 1962)
> First Black Consensus All-American Quarterback (1961)
> Gopher Football National Championship (1960)
> College Back of the Year (1960)
> Rose Bowl (2); MVP (1962)

- 3rd Runner-up for Heisman Trophy (1961)
- University of Minnesota All-Century Team
- Star Tribune 200 All-Century Top Sports Figures (No. 30)
- NCAA Legends status
- Minnesota Top 50 All-Time Athletes
- Halls of Fame

   Gopher Sports Hall of Fame (Class of 1994)
   Rose Bowl Hall of Fame (Class of 1997)
   Western Chapter – Pennsylvania Sports Hall of Fame (1999)
   Star Tribune Minnesota Sports Hall of Fame (Class of 2006)
   Fayette County Sports Hall of Fame (Class of 2009)
   Pennsylvania Sports Hall of Fame (Class of 2010)
   National Football Foundation – College Football Foundation
      Hall of Fame (Class of 2011)
   Uniontown Academic, Arts, & Athletics Hall of Fame (Class of 2013)

Professional Recognitions:

- ❖ Drafted by 3 Professional football teams – 1st Round - AFL (American Football League), New York Titans [now Jets]; and CFL (Canadian Football League), Montreal Alouettes; 2nd round - NFL (National Football League), Cleveland Browns (1962)
- ❖ Quarterback for CFL Teams – Montreal Alouettes and Toronto Argonauts (1962-1963)

Unreached: Goals and Aspirations

- ❖ Long-Term Analyst – Midwest Sports Channel – U of MN Football
- ❖ Ventures International Productions
- ❖ COAST International import/export success
- ❖ Promotion of a Black College Football Classic
- ❖ Development of a Rural Community Cellular Service
- ❖ Acquisition of funding for the *Fountain of Love Institution for World Peace Through Love*

APPENDIX D

Selected Sports Recommendations:

1. *Third and A Mile, The Trials and Triumphs of the Black Quarterback, An Oral History* by William C. Rhoden, ESPN Books, 2007 http://www.espnbooks.com/.
2. *University of Minnesota's First Black Quarterback, Sandy Stephens* / African American Registry / http://www.aaregistry.org/.
3. Sandy Stephens to be honored Saturday; Late Gopher QB will be inducted into College Football Hall of Fame later this year. http://www.cstv.com.
4. *Sports Legends, A History of Minnesota Sports* by Phil Tippin, and Randy Shaver. D Media, Inc., 2008.
5. *Memory Lane* by George Von Benko, 2011.
6. *Gopher Glory, The Pride of the Maroon & Gold* by Jim Burton, KCI Sports Publishing, 2009.
7. *"M" Club Hall of Fame, Class of 2007* by Ross Bernstein, Bernstein Books, 2007, http://www.bernsteinbooks.com.
8. *Pigskin Pride, Celebrating a Century of Minnesota Football* by Ross Bernstein, Nodin Press, 2000.
9. *The Golden Leader – Sandy Stephens – Minnesota Football* http://www.bigten.org/genrel/021808aab.html.
10. Encyclopedia > Sandy Stephens, http://www.nationmaster.com/encyclopedia/Sandy-Stephens
11. *Gold is Also Black, The Story of a Black Quarterback, Tony Brown's Journal*, 1979.
12. *Gopher Gold, Legendary Figures, Brilliant Blunders, and Amazing Feats at the University of Minnesota* by Tim Brady.
13. *A Human Tackling Dummy: How I Helped the Gophers Go to the Rose Bowl,* Essay by David Butwin, Minnesota, U of MN Alumni Association.

Printed in the United States
By Bookmasters